The Complete Guide to Hunting Wild Boar in California

The Complete Guide to Hunting Wild Boar in California

by
Gary Kramer

SAFARI PRESS INC.

Kramer, G.

First edition

Safari Press Inc.

2003, Long Beach, California

ISBN 1-57157-269-4

Library of Congress Catalog Card Number: 2002109356

10 9 8 7 6 5 4 3 2 1

Readers wishing to receive the Safari Press catalog, featuring many fine books on big-game hunting, wingshooting, and sporting firearms, should write to Safari Press Inc., P.O. Box 3095, Long Beach, CA 90803, USA. Tel: (714) 894-9080 or visit our Web site at www.safaripress.com.

To Robert and Louise Kramer

Table of Contents

Foreword

Wild boars did not originate on these shores, but there is no doubt that they have become an all-American favorite of big-game hunters. The single overriding factor that has allowed the immigrant swine to root their way onto the short list with deer, elk, and bears is opportunity. The hogs are plenty wary, elusive, formidable, and can even become a bit testy. Their trophy aspect is, perhaps, an eye-of-the-beholder virtue, but there's no arguing about the pork—a prime, eating-size wild pig makes for a mighty good barbecue.

For all these reasons, many of us who live in states not yet gone-to-the-hogs are seeking the aforementioned opportunity, and there is no better place than in California, which, for various reasons, is not customarily high on the list of hunters' destinations. This brings us to this much-needed new book and why I believe it will serve as a valuable guide not only for Californians eying a consumptive connection with homegrown natural resources, but for sportsmen across the nation as well.

When folks in my line of work need the "raw materials"—in our case, words and photographs—for articles on any type of Pacific Coast hunting, there are just a couple of expert sources we seek out, and foremost among them is the author of this book, Gary Kramer. Indeed, if Gary doesn't have slide-sheets full of spectacular images in his photo library and insightful hunting commentary on a given subject, that critter's probably gone the way of the great golden bear. A California native, career wildlife professional, and lifelong outdoorsman, Gary is eminently qualified to hold forth on this complicated state's "hidden assets." Gary's journalistic style tends to the utilitarian and is unflinchingly thorough. He never fails to tell his readers where, when, how, who, and sometimes why—all the details one needs to know to follow in his footsteps. His camera is just as sharp and all-seeing. The combination of these communicative skills is clearly evident and presented with great advantage in this book. No stone remains unturned—readers surely will find themselves fully prepared to chase a compelling game animal through an equally spectacular landscape.

John Zent
Editor, *American Hunter*
August 16, 2002

Preface

It seems a bit unlikely that a kid from the suburbs of Los Angeles, California, would end up with a career that dealt with wildlife and hunting. From my earliest recollections, however, I have always been interested in the outdoors and animals. Even though there were not many wild places near Los Angeles in the 1960s when I grew up, I still managed to find a few sparrows and jack rabbits to shoot with my pellet gun. My hunting grounds were vacant lots and Los Angeles Airport property before it was fully developed and turned into runways. Needless to say, the airport police didn't appreciate calls from pilots about two kids with guns at the end of the runway. It's amazing that my buddy Vince Bruccolieri and I only got caught once!

My grandfather, Karl Kramer, introduced me to the outdoors— not to hunting but to saltwater fishing off Redondo Beach and Santa Monica. As I was growing up, I found myself drawn to magazines like *Outdoor Life* and *Sports Afield* rather than the more traditional boys' fare of comic books and super heroes. By the time I was in high school and could drive, I had developed a genuine interest in the outdoors, so my weekends were spent shooting jack rabbits in the Antelope Valley or hunting doves in the Imperial Valley.

It was during high school that I became interested in big-game hunting. My first successful deer hunt was in the 1960s when Larry Rauen and I drew deer tags for Fort Hunter Liggett Military Reservation in Monterey County. Not only did we shoot our first deer, but we also saw our first wild hogs. Before long, we were chasing hogs. It took a few trips and lots of legwork, but I finally killed my first wild boar in San Luis Obispo County in the late 1960s.

I enrolled in El Camino College after high school, and promptly flunked out of zoology and received a "D" in English. You might say I wasn't quite ready for college! Looking back, I find it ironic that I did poorly in the two subjects that would form the cornerstones of my chosen career. About that time, things were heating up in Vietnam, and as a nineteen-year-old without a student deferment I was fodder for the draft. So instead of being drafted into the army, I joined the navy. Joining the navy seemed like my best option until my ship steamed into Da Nang harbor. I eventually returned home safely and enrolled at Humboldt State University. In 1974, I graduated with a B.S. degree in wildlife management. I received my M.S. in wildlife management in 1976. Jobs were hard to find, but I landed a wildlife-biologist position with the Bureau of Land Management in Ely, Nevada. After eighteen months, I transferred to the U.S. Fish and Wildlife Service. My duty station was the Kern National Wildlife Refuge, northwest of Bakersfield.

It was about that time (late 1970s) that I wrote my first outdoor story. It appeared in *Western Outdoors* magazine and was on brant hunting at San Quintin Bay in Baja California, which had been the subject of my master's degree a few years before. Bob Robb, then editor of *Western Outdoor News*, can be credited for getting me interested in outdoor writing, and he was instrumental in helping me publish my first article. It wasn't long until a second article was published, and I was on my way to a second career in outdoor writing.

In the meantime, my career with the U.S. Fish and Wildlife Service progressed, and I moved from Kern to the San Luis Refuge in Los Banos. In 1984, I was selected to manage the Salton Sea National Wildlife Refuge—a dry, hot place I already knew from my early dove-hunting days in the Imperial Valley. My writing expanded to include hunting trips to Argentina and Canada and fishing trips to Mexico and Alaska. I had the best of both worlds: I was involved on a daily basis in wildlife conservation, and I moonlighted as an outdoor writer and photographer.

In 1989 I transferred to the Sacramento National Wildlife Refuge, near Willows, as the manager. From the beginning, working at Sacramento Refuge was my dream job. While I was attending classes at Humboldt State, I had gone on a field trip to Sacramento Refuge. On the field trip, I made a comment that someday I would like to work there. Little did I know that fifteen years later I would not only work there but also run the place as the refuge manager. About that time as well, my secondary writing and photography career escalated, and I began to travel more and more, often to exotic places like Botswana, Iceland, Uruguay, and Russia. I was writing regularly for *The Hunting Report*, *The Bird Hunting Report*, *Shooting Sportsman*, *Outdoor Life*, *American Hunter*, and other national publications. I had the best of both worlds, but it was a busy time.

In 1999 the opportunity for early retirement from the U.S. Fish and Wildlife Service became available, and, after plenty of soul searching, I gave up my day job. In August 1999 I retired. After twenty-six years with the government, most of it in wildlife management, and at age fifty-one, I embarked on a full-time writing and photo career. I had enjoyed the National Wildlife Refuge System and the people I worked with, and I was satisfied that I had done the best job possible throughout my career. However, it was time to move on.

One of the first things that came up was an offer to write a book on California wild-pig hunting. I had written a story on that subject in *The Hunting Report*, and Safari Press publisher Ludo Wurfbain called to ask if I would consider writing a book on pig hunting. I told him I appreciated the offer but that I wasn't the world's expert on hog hunting, and, further, I didn't have time to write a book. A year later we discussed the project again, and in 2001 I started on the book. I'll be the first to admit that I have not shot a hundred wild pigs, nor have I been a hog-hunting guide. However, I have put the cross hairs on my share of wild hogs, and most of them have hit the ground when I pulled the trigger. After doing the research and writing this book, I now know more about wild-pig hunting than I did before, and I am a better hunter for it. It is my hope that sharing with my readers the hunting experiences and insights I have gathered over the past thirty-five years will help to make them better hog hunters as well.

Acknowledgments

Writing a book, particularly for the first time, is a monumental undertaking. It takes perseverance and research, and, in the case of this project, it was necessary to contact a variety of individuals—from biologists to hunting guides. Without their help, this book would not have been possible. First, I would like to thank the many hunting guides I interviewed. By and large, they were honest in their answers and, in most cases, tried to give me an accurate "feel" for the type of operations they ran. I would particularly like to thank Wayne and Gordy Long of Multiple Use Managers (Dye Creek Preserve), Rick Copeland of Wilderness Unlimited, and August Harden of Cross Country Outfitters for providing insight into their hunting operations. I would also like to thank Cristen Langner with the California Department of Fish and Game, who reviewed the natural history and public land portions of the manuscript, and Dave Paullin, a friend and expert hunter, who reviewed the weapons and equipment sections.

I also would like to thank Ludo Wurfbain for persuading me to write this book in the first place and for encouraging me along the way. Additionally I would like to thank Judy Taylor, my office assistant, who took care of the everyday office work so that I was free to concentrate on the creative aspects of my job.

Finally I would like to thank my family: my wife, Eileen, who has always been patient and understanding of my long absences, not only during the course of writing this book but also during the entire twenty-nine years we have been married. I would like to thank my daughters, Elaine and Kelly, for also being understanding and accepting of my frequent absences.

Introduction

Given that I'm a native of California, it's not surprising that one of the first big-game animals I harvested was a wild pig. My interest in hunting wild hogs actually began during my first successful deer hunt back in the 1960s while I was still in high school. My hunting buddy Larry Rauen and I drew deer tags for Fort Hunter Liggett Military Reservation in Monterey County, and on that hunt we saw our first hogs. It wasn't long before we began chasing hogs around the state. It took several trips and lots of legwork, but I finally killed my first wild boar in San Luis Obispo County in the late 1960s. Today, more than thirty years later, I still find hog hunting a challenging and rewarding experience.

While total hunting-license sales in California have dropped over the past decade and the number of deer tags sold has steadily declined, the number of wild-pig hunters has increased. The inevitable question is why? The primary reason has to do with the number of wild hogs and the hunting opportunities available. In contrast to deer populations, which have been on a decline for years, wild-hog populations have been increasing and their range expanding

Because wild hogs can be hunted year-long, are numerous on private land, and afford relatively close shots under the right conditions, they are tailor-made for new hunters, both adults and kids. (All photographs are by Gary Kramer unless otherwise noted.)

since the 1960s. In 1998, for the first time since the California Department of Fish and Game (CDF&G) began keeping records of the annual harvest, the number of wild pigs killed exceeded the number of deer taken, making wild hogs California's number one big-game animal. Based on estimates by the CDF&G, wild-pig hunters in California spend about twenty-five million dollars annually on their sport.

For years you could hunt wild pigs merely by possessing a valid hunting license. Today, tags are required for wild pigs, but compared to deer tags, hog tags are easy to obtain and can be purchased over the counter. Another attraction of pig hunting is the year-round season. In contrast to deer, elk, and pronghorns, which have relatively short seasons, hog hunting can be enjoyed every month of the year.

And one more attraction: Wild-pig hunting is just plain fun. In areas where they are abundant, hogs are relatively easy to locate, and, generally, you don't have to devote a week of hard hunting to kill a nice one. It can often be accomplished in a day or a weekend, particularly on private land. Additionally, wild pigs are a great choice for those new to big-game hunting. Because they can be hunted all year, are numerous on private land, and afford relatively close shots under the right conditions, they are tailor-made for new hunters, both adults and kids. In fact, my daughter's first big-game animal was a nice meat pig she killed on the Dye Creek Preserve a few years ago. Finally, wild hogs are excellent table fare—in fact, many hunters put a 125-pound wild pig among the best eating of all the game animals. For all these reasons and others, wild-hog hunting has become the Golden State's fastest-growing big-game opportunity. In the following pages, we'll take a close look at pig hunting in California, and you'll soon see why this area of big-game hunting has turned into a bonanza.

The hogs in California, and the rest of the United States, are a mixture of domestic pigs gone wild and true European wild pigs, like this boar.

Wild Pig Distribution
in California

Chapter 1

Natural History and Distribution

The wild pig (*Sus scrofa*) is native to Europe, North Africa, and portions of western and central Asia. The first documented introduction of pure-strain European wild pigs in the United States occurred in 1890, when Austin Corbin imported thirteen animals from the Black Forest of Germany and placed them in a fenced game preserve in New Hampshire. Introductions continued well into the 1900s, with European-strain wild hogs liberated in Alabama, California, Tennessee, and several other states. These animals—along with domestic pigs gone wild and their crosses—have evolved into the wild or feral pigs we find today in the United States. Wild pigs have become established in at least twenty-one states, including Alabama, Arizona, Arkansas, California, Florida, Georgia, Hawaii, Iowa, Kentucky, Louisiana, Mississippi, Missouri, New Mexico, North Carolina, Oklahoma, Oregon, South Carolina, Tennessee, Texas, Virginia, and West Virginia.

The hogs in California today, as in the remainder of the United States, are a mixture of domestic pigs gone wild and true European wild pigs. Feral hogs have been present in California since the arrival of the Spanish in the 1500s. Their numbers increased in the 1700s, when additional animals were brought in by European settlers. Historians indicate that domestic pigs were often allowed to forage in the state's oak woodlands to take advantage of the acorn crops. Some pigs escaped and created wild, free-ranging populations. After 1850, as new settlements and homesteads spread throughout the state in the wake of the Gold Rush, domestic swine were commonly released, expanding their distribution even farther.

In late 1925, pure-strain European or Russian wild hogs were brought into California from Hooper Bald, North Carolina, where they were descendants of the original New Hampshire introduction.

Some of the best wild-pig habitat is in the coast range from Humboldt County in the north to Santa Barbara County in the south. Mendocino County is typical north-coast, wild-pig habitat, a mixture of annual grasslands, oak woodland, and conifers.

This is an aerial view of Santa Rosa Island. In the late 1980s, the National Park Service purchased Santa Rosa Island from the Val and Vickers Company, who had owned the island since 1902. Wild hogs were found to have a detrimental impact on the island's endangered plants and animals, so they were eradicated from Santa Rosa.

Under a game breeder's permit, these hogs were transported into Monterey County by George Gordon Moore and released on what is now the San Carlos Ranch in Carmel Valley. Shortly thereafter, Stuyvesant Fish, owner of the neighboring Palo Carona ranch, obtained several of the European hogs from Moore's property and released them on his place. From these two ranches European wild hogs spread south into the Santa Lucia Mountains, where they bred with the established feral-hog population and produced offspring with characteristics of both European hogs and feral stock. Since that time, European-strain wild pigs and their progeny have been liberated in Monterey, San Luis Obispo, Fresno, San Benito, Mendocino, Shasta, and Tehama counties.

Today, wild pigs occur in California's coast range in hardwood, chaparral, riparian, and grassland habitat types from Humboldt County in the north to Santa Barbara County in the south. To a lesser degree they are found throughout most of the lower elevations of the western Sierra Nevada foothills from Shasta County to the Tehachapi Mountains in Kern County. Other populations exist in Siskiyou, Modoc, San Bernardino, Riverside, Ventura, and Los Angeles counties. (See distribution map.)

Wild pigs are expanding their range in California. Until the mid-1960s, their numbers were relatively low and their distribution limited, with the largest populations occurring in the north and central coast ranges. Since then wild hogs have dispersed into new areas where forage conditions were good. By the mid-1980s, the state's hog population was estimated at 100,000 animals. Currently, wild pigs inhabit an estimated 26,000 square miles of habitat and exist in at least fifty-three of the state's fifty-eight counties. Indications are that their range is still expanding. The CDF&G currently estimates the statewide population at 130,000 animals.

The story is different on California's offshore islands. Formerly, there were good wild-hog populations on Santa Rosa and Santa Cruz off the central coast and Catalina and San Clemente islands off the south coast. Both guided and unguided hunts were available on three of the islands. However, in recent years things have changed drastically.

In the late 1980s, the National Park Service (NPS) purchased Santa Rosa Island from the Val and Vickers Company, which had owned

Wild hogs are about three feet high at the shoulder and are covered with stiff, bristly hairs that are predominantly black or brown.

the island since 1902. NPS policy required removing nonnative species from parklands. Further, wild hogs were having a detrimental impact on the island's endangered plants and animals. As a result, wild pigs have been eradicated from Santa Rosa. Santa Cruz Island, owned jointly by The Nature Conservancy (TNC) and NPS, still supports wild pigs. In the past, controlled hunts were allowed. The last hunt took place in the spring of 2002, but there are no plans for future public pig hunts. The NPS, in cooperation with TNC, plans to eradicate the hogs on Santa Cruz in the next five years.

Wild hogs still exist on Catalina Island, but in low numbers. Since the early 1990s, pigs have been removed by the Catalina Conservancy, which owns most of the island, in an effort to minimize the damage the hogs were causing to range land and endangered species. The U.S. Navy uses San Clemente as a bombing range. In the early 1980s, the navy began removing hogs from the island at the rate of up to three hundred per year. A few pigs remain on San Clemente.

There's no question that the density of hogs present in a given area is a key factor in hunter success. In California, biologists define high density as more than ten hogs per one hundred acres; five to nine per hundred acres is moderate, and fewer than four hogs per hundred acres is low density. California's high-density areas include Mendocino, Santa Clara, and Sonoma counties on the north coast and San Benito, Monterey, and San Luis Obispo counties on the central coast. Additionally, high-density pockets exist in Tehama, Kings, Santa Barbara, Shasta, and Colusa counties.

In California, under optimal habitat conditions, the home range of a particular hog or group of hogs is generally ten square miles or less. When food is in short supply, wild hogs may range over an area as extensive as fifty square miles. Within each home range there are one or more "core areas" where the combination of food, water, and cover is optimal. Hogs spend a lot of time in these core areas.

Wild hogs stand about three feet high at the shoulder and are covered with stiff, bristly hairs that are predominantly black or brown. Individuals more closely related to domestic pigs may display color variations ranging from pure black to blond and numerous color combinations including two-tone black and white and light or dark spots on a contrasting background. Purebred European boars have a

The band of long hair extending down the back and forming a ridge indicates that this boar has some European ancestry.

band of long hair extending down their back to form a ridge commonly referred to as a "razor back"—thus the name "razorback hog." They are "split-hoofed" animals and leave a track similar to a deer's but more rounded. Their sight is poor, but their hearing and smell are acute. All pigs have a naked, fleshy snout used to root out bulbs, roots, nuts, and insects. Patches of disturbed ground are a sure sign that hogs are using an area. Droppings are elongated and look similar to a string of sausages.

Males have enlarged canine teeth or "tusks" that, in the larger boars, protrude from the mouth. A boar with tusks longer than two

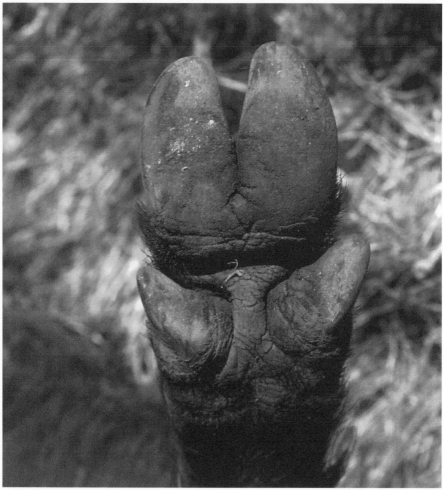

Wild hogs are "split-toed" animals. The tracks of large hogs leave the imprint of both the hoof and dew claw.

The tracks of wild hogs are similar to those of a deer, but more rounded.

inches (measured from the gum line) is considered a trophy and stands a good chance of making it to the taxidermist. A boar with tusks three inches or longer is a rarity and would fall into the upper 5 percent of the pigs taken annually in California. Wild hogs are omnivorous, feeding on insects, acorns, wild fruit, grass, carrion, and agricultural crops including small grains, truck crops, pasture grasses, alfalfa, and domestic fruits. They have been known to capture and kill small prey including rabbits, snakes, lizards, and frogs, and they never pass up the eggs of ground-nesting birds. In some areas they cause extensive damage to crops, ornamentals, gardens, and lawns and can be a menace on golf courses, where they tear up fairways and greens while rooting out bulbs, grubs, and insects.

While the breeding season in California is year-round, mating activity peaks in the spring and again in the fall, with sows dropping young after a four-month gestation period. Two litters per year are common, and sows generally have four to eight young per litter, though births can number up to fourteen. One study in Tehama County showed an average litter size of five to six piglets. At birth, the young average one to three pounds and are often striped in coloration. Wild hogs grow fast—young females are capable of reproduction at six to ten months of age and may weigh less than a hundred pounds. Older and larger females generally produce larger litters.

Diet has a profound influence on breeding success. When food is abundant and nutritional, piglet production and survival are high. A good example occurred during the 1987 to 1992 droughts, when precipitation in California averaged 76 percent of normal. During that period, wild-hog production and harvest dropped nearly 50 percent from previous years. The poor precipitation patterns resulted in poor plant growth and low insect populations, and hog survival suffered. In contrast, a series of wet years in the late 1990s resulted in high production and survival of young, low overall mortality, and excellent hunter success.

Sows and piglets live in family groups, which may merge with others to form herds of fifty or more animals in some areas. Males generally travel alone or in bachelor groups, joining the families during the breeding season. Wild hogs are most active at dawn and dusk and in some areas, particularly where they are heavily hunted or harassed, adopt nocturnal behavior patterns. During the day they seek shade and often visit wallows, where they roll to coat their bodies with mud for its cooling effect and to ward off insects. They communicate by grunts and squeals similar to those of domestic pigs.

Wild hogs come in all shapes and sizes, but the live weight of most adults is 100 to 200 pounds, with a few exceptionally large boars tipping the scales at more than 400 pounds. Typically, boars weigh about 25 percent more than similar-age sows using the same habitat. Characteristically, wild hogs are relatively lean animals, and reports of 600-pounders are probably triggered by domestic animals released into the wild, not by wild stock that has been at large for several generations. A Tehama County study listed the largest boar harvested at 375 pounds, while reports of 450-pound boars on the central coast have been verified. Still, even a 300-pound jet-black wild boar with three-inch tusks is an awesome sight to behold!

Chapter 2

Preparing For The Hunt

Licensing Requirements and Regulations

Prior to 1957, wild pigs were considered vermin. They were unclassified under state law and thus unprotected; consequently, a hunting license was not required, and hogs could be killed by any means and in any number at any time. In 1957 the wild hog was classified as a game animal by the California legislature. The Fish and Game Commission set seasons and bag limits according to the goals established by the legislature, and hunters needed a license to pursue wild pigs. Since that time the season has been yearlong, and until 1996 there was a bag and possession limit of one or two pigs daily, depending on the area hunted. In 1996 the Fish and Game Commission adopted regulations eliminating the bag and possession limit.

In 1992 the Commission began requiring any person twelve years of age or older (the legal California big-game hunting age minimum)

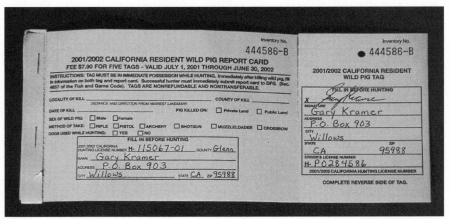

In 1992, the Fish and Game Commission adopted regulations requiring any person twelve years of age or older to possess wild-pig tags while hunting. Both portions of the tag must be partially filled out prior to hunting.

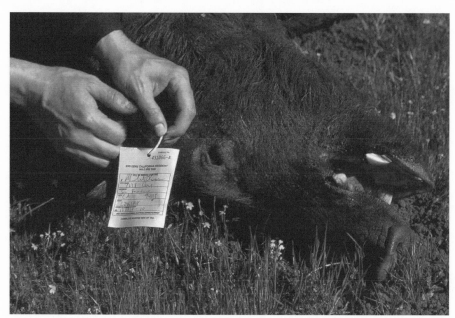

Once an animal is killed, the hunter must finish filling out the tag portion by clearly marking the date, location, time of kill, and the sex of the pig. The hunter then attaches it to the carcass.

to possess wild-pig tags while hunting. Both portions of the tag must be partially filled out prior to hunting. Once an animal is killed, the hunter must finish filling out the tag by clearly marking the date, location, time of kill, and the sex of the pig; he then must attach the tag to the carcass. The report-card portion must be filled out and immediately returned to the CDF&G. Wild-pig tags are sold to residents in packets of five and to nonresidents individually. Pig tags can be purchased at CDF&G offices and license agents (most sporting-goods stores, Wal-Mart, etc.). They are valid only during a portion of the current hunting-license year. For example, a pig tag bought in January is good only until the hunting-license year ends on June 30. The requirement was adopted to allow the CDF&G to obtain basic wild-pig harvest information and to provide funding for management.

Wild pigs are classified as big game in California and, consequently, can be taken only with:

1) rifles or pistols using centerfire cartridges with softnose or expanding bullets;
2) bow and arrow including crossbows;

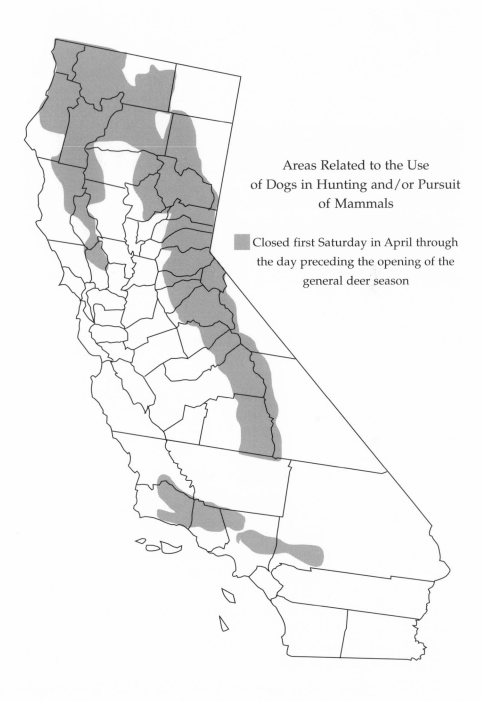

Areas Related to the Use
of Dogs in Hunting and/or Pursuit
of Mammals

Closed first Saturday in April through
the day preceding the opening of the
general deer season

3) muzzleloading rifles using black or Pyrodex powder with a single ball or bullet of at least .40 caliber loaded from the muzzle, and a barrel measuring twenty-six inches or more in length equipped with iron sights only;

4) shotguns capable of holding no more than three shells firing single slugs.

Archers seeking big game, including hogs, must use hunting arrows or crossbow bolts with a broadhead blade that will not pass through a hole seven-eighths of an inch in diameter. Explosive heads or arrows that tranquilize or poison are prohibited. The bow or crossbow must be capable of casting a legal hunting arrow a horizontal distance of 130 yards.

The use of dogs in wild-hog hunting is widespread. Certain portions of California are open all year to the use of dogs for the pursuit of wild hogs or for dog-training purposes. In other areas (dog-control zones), the use of dogs for pig and other mammal hunting is prohibited from the first Saturday in April through the day preceding the opening of the general deer season. Additionally, no more than three dogs per hunter can be used to hunt pigs, and no more than one dog per hunter is legal during the general deer season. (Note dog control zone map.)

Additional information, including the cost of licenses and tags, can be obtained from a regional or field office of the CDF&G.

CDF&G Regional Offices

Northern California and North Coast Region
601 Locust St.
Redding, CA 96001
530-225-2300

Sacramento Valley and Central Sierra Region
1701 Nimbus Rd.
Rancho Cordova, CA 95670
916-358-2900

Central Coast Region

7329 Silverado Trail

Napa, CA 94558

707-944-5500

San Joaquin Valley and Southern Sierra Region

1234 East Shaw Ave.

Fresno, CA 93710

559-243-4005

South Coast Region

4949 Viewridge Ave.

San Diego, CA 92123

858-467-4201

Eastern Sierra and Inland Region

4775 Bird Farm Rd.

Chino Hills, CA

909-597-9823

Field Offices

Eureka

619 Second St.

Eureka, CA 95501

707-445-6493

Belmont

355 Harbor Blvd.

Belmont, CA 94002

650-631-7730

Los Alamitos

4665 Lampson Ave., Suite C

Los Alamitos, CA 90720

562-342-7100

Monterey
Lower Ragsdale Dr., #100
Monterey, CA 93940
831-649-2870

License and Revenue Branch
3211 S St.
Sacramento, CA 95816
916-227-2177

CDF&G Web site: www.dfg.ca.gov

Rifles and Pistols; Calibers and Bullets

Beyond the requirement that a centerfire rifle or pistol cartridge be used to hunt pigs, the selection of weapon, caliber, and bullet is up to you. Among modern sporting rifles, the bolt-action is by far the most popular. However, plenty of hunters armed with lever-action, semiautomatic, pump-action, and single-shot rifles have killed their share of wild pigs. Bolt-action rifles come in more makes and models than any other type and can be chambered for virtually any cartridge available. Add nearly foolproof cartridge feeding and a positive bolt lock, and you can see why this action has become popular. And with the advent of synthetic stocks and lighter barrels, the weight of bolt-action rifles has come down as well.

According to longtime firearms expert and hunter Craig Boddington, whatever rifle you have the most confidence in is the right choice. Most of the advantages one action type may have over another are more theoretical than actual. The bolt-action rifle in the hands of an experienced shooter tends to be only slightly more accurate than a semiautomatic, lever-action, or pump. Just about any hunting scenario for wild pigs can be adequately addressed with any of the action types available today.

Highly popular, too, are telescopic sights. Fifty years ago, scopes were the exception rather than the rule, and iron sights were still the way to go for most big-game hunting. Today, however, you will see very few rifles in the field that are not topped with a scope. And it's no wonder, given recent advances in optics. You can buy variable-power scopes, scopes with built-in range finders, scopes with a variety of reticles, and scopes designed for low-light situations and even for rain. Scopes have become an essential part of our hunting equipment, and rightfully so. They magnify the target, provide a single sight plane (you don't have to line up front and rear sights), and gather light to present a clearer sight picture of your quarry early in the morning and at dusk—the two periods when hogs are most active and most are shot.

Like rifle actions, you're the boss when it comes to selecting the brand, power, and fixed-power versus variable model. I prefer a 3–9X or 2–7X variable. Either allows the user to vary the degree of magnification to suit the shooting scenario. The 7X or 9X setting might be used for a long shot in open terrain early in the morning or on a cool day when heat-wave interference is minimal. The identical shot in the same location at midday or in August, when the heat waves make it tough to get an accurate sight picture at higher magnification, might require the use of a 5X or 6X setting. The 2X and 3X settings might be used in heavy cover when hogs are close and bedded down in deep shade. If you prefer a fixed-power model rather than a variable, I'd recommend a 4X for general-purpose hunting and a 6X if most of your hunting is in open country.

Caliber choice is the most-discussed topic among that segment of pig hunters characterized as "gun nuts." The law allows any centerfire cartridge to be used for big game, but seasoned hunters, outfitters, and guides unanimously recommend .243 caliber or larger for pig hunting. Anything smaller just doesn't pack enough punch to consistently kill pigs. Wild boars in particular are notorious for taking well-placed shots that would drop most animals in their tracks. Hogs can take a good hit and keep on going! They are more difficult to kill than deer, antelope, or other similar-size, soft-skinned quarry.

On the other end of the spectrum are the larger calibers, anything above .340 caliber—the .350 Remington Magnum, .375 Winchester, and the like. These big boys will certainly stop pigs dead in their tracks, but the tradeoffs include excessive recoil (particularly with the magnums), loss of accuracy due to bullet drop at long ranges, and, in my opinion, hunter fatigue from carrying around more firepower than the situation calls for.

Longtime pig hunters like Gordy Long, who manages Dye Creek Preserve and has killed or guided hunters to literally thousands of hogs, swears by the .30-06. He claims it is flat-shooting enough for most situations and is accurate in the hands of most shooters out to two hundred yards. Further, the customary 150- or 180-grain bullet packs enough punch to cleanly kill both meat hogs in the 100- to 150-pound range and trophy boars topping 300 pounds. That said, Gordy also recommends the .270 Winchester, 7mm Remington Magnum, .308 Winchester, and .300 Winchester Magnum. Most hunting at Dye Creek is in open to wooded country, and the shots can sometimes be long.

Next to calibers, you can spend hours debating the attributes of one bullet type and weight over another. And no wonder: The bullet is the device that ultimately puts the game on the ground. For hogs, most experts agree that in the smaller calibers like the .243, it is best to go with the heaviest bullets commonly available. For the .243 Winchester it's a 100-grain bullet, for the .257 Roberts it's 100 grains, and for the .25-06 Remington it's 120 grains. Once you move into the medium calibers, heavier bullets are available.

Hunters who make their shots from less than 75 yards may find revolvers—both single and double action—effective. Jim Settle used a .44-caliber Ruger revolver on this trophy boar.

In these calibers it's generally best to stay with bullets that fall in the center of the available weights. For example, the 130-grain .270 bullet is preferred over a lighter bullet, and in .30 caliber, the 150- to 165-grain bullets are better than lighter ones. The lighter bullets are designed for soft-skinned and smaller game like varmints, not thick-skinned, harder-to-kill animals like wild hogs. Some hunters go to the heavier bullets where there is lots of brush and the shooting distances are relatively short. The 180- or 200-grain bullet in .30 caliber would fall into this category.

Bullet types are another area of debate. Sierra Boattail, Nosler Partition, Winchester Silvertip, Federal Premium, Remington Silvertip, or Hornady Interlock—they are all designed to reach the target, penetrate the skin, expand, and cause enough damage to put the animal down quickly. Outfitters like August Harden of Cross Country Outfitters, who sees literally hundreds of hogs killed each year, feel that the Winchester Fail Safe, Barnes X-Bullet, and Swift A-Frame are the best wild-pig bullets on the market today. Harden believes the type of bullet is even more important than its weight or the caliber. Again, the choice of bullet weight and type usually comes down to confidence and personal preference. If you have a bolt-action .270 that you feel comfortable shooting, and you consistently kill deer or other big game with it using a 130-grain Fail Safe, then that's the rifle and load you should use for wild pigs.

What about pistols? There are single-shot, revolver, semiautomatic, and even bolt-action hunting handguns. If you are going to hunt hogs with a pistol and essentially spot-and-stalk them (no dogs), a flat-shooting model with a barrel at least six inches long is recommended. Single-shot models are the Thompson/Center Contender, Thompson Encore, and Magnum Research Lone Eagle. All are single-action handguns designed for hunting and are built for accuracy at ranges beyond the capability of most pistols. These handguns are available in calibers you would expect to find in rifles, including the .260 Remington, .300 Savage, .308 Winchester, and others. Using these special weapons topped with scopes, some hunters consistently kill big game out to two hundred yards with the proper rest. For shots less than seventy-five yards, many hunters find single- and double-action revolvers made by Ruger, Freedom Arms, Magnum Research, and others very effective.

When hunting pigs with dogs, most shots are at close range and are accompanied by the chaos of barking dogs and a squealing pig. This situation at times allows the use of shorter barrels and either semiautomatic or revolver actions. More than one shot may need to be delivered in rapid succession, hence the need for a repeating-action firearm.

Hog pistols generally fall into the .40-caliber category. Pistol cartridges have less muzzle velocity than rifle cartridges, but the deficit is partially overcome by increasing the caliber and weight of the bullet. Because pistol packers generally shoot pigs at relatively close range, the heavier bullets and their inherent propensity to drop as the distance increases are not as much of a factor as with rifles. Therefore, the .44 Smith & Wesson with 200-grain bullets, the .44 Remington Magnum with 240-grain bullets, and the .50 Action Express with 325-grain bullets are popular pistol combinations for pigs.

Many handgun hunters, particularly those with dogs, use the factory-fitted open sights. However, if spot-and-stalk hunting is your choice, a handgun with a scope is a good bet. A 2X scope is sufficient in most close-in scenarios, but in open country or mixed habitats a variable scope is a better choice. Most veteran handgun hunters use a 2–6X or 2–7X. A rest is always a good idea.

Shotguns

Data from the CDF&G show that in 2000, only 2 percent of the wild hogs killed in California were taken with shotguns.

Most of those were killed on controlled hunting areas where the use of shotguns was mandatory. As with rifles, the type of shotgun and action—semiautomatic, pump, double barrel, or single barrel—is your call. Most shotgun-toting pig hunters use autos or pumps, preferring their ability to hold and deliver three rounds. Serious shotgunners use barrels that have open sights and are designed for slugs. Most hunters use 12-gauge shotguns, a few use 10-gauge, and even fewer use 20-gauge weapons. In all cases, regulations require the use of single slugs and shotguns that can hold no more than three shells. Shotgun-slug hunters should keep their shots under seventy-five yards, and fifty yards is even better.

Black-Powder Weapons

In recent years the number of big-game animals harvested across the United States with black-powder weapons has skyrocketed. In California alone, it is estimated that more than 10,000 hunters own muzzleloading rifles and spend at least a few days a year in the field shooting them. Much of the rise in popularity is a result of special big-game seasons for black-powder weapons only. Deer are the main targets of smokepole users. Because hogs can be hunted year-round and there are no special black-powder pig hunts in California, the incentive to hunt them with muzzleloaders is just not there. Nonetheless, hunting hogs with muzzleloaders can be exciting. For one thing, the critters lend themselves well to black-powder hunting. Given their relatively poor eyesight, a hunter who approaches from downwind and uses existing cover well can get within fifty to seventy-five yards of most pigs—perfect distances for black-powder weapons. With the right powder charge and bullet weight, shots of a hundred yards are possible.

Muzzleloading rifles are available today in seemingly endless varieties, including flintlocks, sidelocks, and in-line models. Of course, the action type, caliber, bullet weight, and even type of bullet are subjects of debate among black-powder aficionados. The most popular combos are .50- and .54-caliber models firing conical or saboted bullets at least 230 grains in weight. The .45 Magnum in-line driving PowerBelts or sabots has enough knockdown power to be surprisingly effective on longer shots at wild hogs. For in-close shooting (fifty yards or less) .54- or .58-caliber round balls are effective.

Archery Equipment

Less than 8 percent of the wild hogs killed annually in California are taken with archery equipment. Like black-powder hunters, archers need to get in close. Wild hogs are low to the ground, and their vital organs are a relatively small target. To hit this area and consistently kill wild hogs with a bow, the shot should be forty yards or less. Some bow hunters feel comfortable shooting at distances beyond forty yards and regularly make clean kills. However, these distances are beyond the capability of most archers.

Data from the California Department of Fish and Game show that less than 8 percent of the wild hogs killed annually are taken with archery equipment. Pat Fisher used a compound bow to take this trophy wild boar.

By far the most popular type of bow is the modern compound. These bows have come a long way from the mid-1970s, when they were first introduced and 18 percent let-off (draw-weight reduction at full draw) was considered revolutionary. Today's compound bows have 65 to 80 percent let-off and allow an archer to shoot a 70-pound bow, for example, but hold as little as 15 pounds at full draw. Bows with at least a 60-pound draw weight are recommended for wild-hog hunting. The shafts used most commonly with compound bows are made of either aluminum or carbon fiber. Some archers use "primitive"-type bows—recurves or longbows—and wooden arrows.

State law requires the use of broadheads. The choices for wild-hog hunting are numerous. Among the more popular brands are 125-grain Thunderheads; Muzzy three-blade 125-grain and four-blade 115-grain; Rocky Mountain TI-125; and the one-piece, fixed-blade Steelforce and Magnus.

Crossbows are probably the least-used weapons for pig hunting in California, but some hogs are killed every year with them. The most appropriate crossbows for wild pigs are aluminum bolts and are draw-weight rated at 150 to 175 pounds. The use of broadheads is mandatory.

Safety

Firearms are lethal, and great care needs to be taken while transporting, cleaning, and hunting with them. The ten basic rules of firearm safety are below.

1) Control the direction of the muzzle; do not ever pull a firearm toward you by the muzzle.
2) Identify your target, and be aware of what is behind it.
3) Treat every firearm as if it were loaded.
4) Be sure your barrel is free from any obstruction and that you are using the correct ammunition.
5) Unload all firearms not in use, and carry them unloaded except when actually hunting.
6) Never point a firearm at anything you do not intend to shoot.
7) Never climb a fence or tree or jump a ditch with a loaded firearm.

8) Never shoot a bullet at water or a flat, hard surface.
9) Store firearms and ammunition separately, away from children and careless adults.
10) Do not drink alcohol or take drugs before or while shooting.

Bow hunters have their own set of common sense rules.

1) Because the energy stored in a drawn bow is lethal, make sure your bow and arrows are free from cracks or breaks and the string is not cut or frayed.
2) Always carry broadhead arrows in a strong quiver that fully covers the tips and blades.
3) Identify your target, and be aware of what is behind it.
4) Never shoot an arrow straight up in the air.
5) Never point a drawn bow at anything you do not want to shoot.
6) Never climb a fence without first placing your bow and arrows on the other side, well away from your crossing point.
7) Never carry archery equipment in a vehicle in such a way that a sudden stop could turn them into deadly missiles.
8) Use the correct methods and equipment when stringing a bow.

Other safety considerations relate to fitness, health, and outdoor skills. Before you go pig hunting, consider whether you have the physical fitness required for the strenuous activity involved. Always carry water to avoid dehydration, and dress appropriately to prevent hypothermia. Always take along a compass, maps of the area, and matches. If you get lost, don't panic! Stop and think about your problem. Carefully plan what you are going to do. The general rule is to stay put and build a fire. If you try to find your way out, be sure to mark your path so that you can return to where you started.

Equipment and Clothing

In addition to the proper licenses and tags, weapons, and ammunition, there are other items essential to a pig-hunting trip. Much of what follows is common sense, but it's surprising how many people overlook the importance of proper gear and clothing.

Spotting scopes are pressed into service when an animal needs to be sized up. This is particularly important when hunting trophy boars.

There is no question that one of the most important items is boots. Nothing can ruin a hunt quicker than blisters and sore feet! While there are dozens of brands to choose from, the most important consideration in choosing boots for hunting—or any activity that requires hiking long distances over rough terrain—is proper fit. Equally important is breaking in those new boots. Don't head to the hills in brand-new boots—wear them around the yard and on short hikes before they are pressed into service as your primary hunting footwear. Ankle support is a prime factor in a hunting boot. Choices range from a six-inch boots like Cabela's Trail-Lite Hikers to a ten-inch full-support model like the Rocky Expedition. Also important is the type of sole. Most hunting boots will have Vibram or gripping-style soles. Stay away from work boots or other types with smooth or nongrip soles. Finally, I wouldn't think of buying boots that weren't waterproof. Even heavy dew will make leather boots miserable to walk in for the rest of the day. There are a number of wax preparations and other ways to make boots waterproof, but a built-in Gore-Tex liner is the most popular method.

Volumes have been written on proper clothing, and numerous companies sell quality clothing designed for hunting and other outdoor use. Many hog hunters wear camouflage. Like most mammals, pigs are colorblind, plus their eyesight is poor. However, camo breaks up your outline and can help you get in close. Among the dozens of patterns and styles available, I have found that Realtree's Hardwoods and Advantage Timber work well in California's oak woodlands, where wild pigs are frequently hunted. Blaze orange is not required in California, but its use is a good idea, particularly on public land.

Another consideration in choosing the proper clothing is variable weather conditions. A clear, balmy day can quickly turn cold, wet, and windy, and without some forethought you will be uncomfortable and may risk hypothermia—or worse. The layering idea is the best solution to changing weather conditions. Here's an example of how it works. I recently hunted pigs on the central coast. The early morning hours were cool and clear, but about 10 A.M. a front moved in, the temperature dropped, heavy clouds rolled in off the ocean, and it began to rain. I had a Gore-Tex jacket and was carrying an additional layer of clothing and thus was able to continue the hunt in relative comfort. Waterproof clothing is an important component of the layering system, and on this particular day it kept me not only dry but also warm.

Whether you hunt behind dogs, still-hunt, or spot-and-stalk hogs, there will come a time when you will use binoculars. Someone once said that spot-and-stalk is 90 percent spot and 10 percent stalk. If that's your favorite method, a good binocular is paramount. Binoculars made by Zeiss, Swarovski, and Leica and some of the higher-end Nikon, Bushnell, and Canon models are well worth the extra money they cost. Most guides and hunters who use a binocular on a regular basis prefer the roof-prism type, which produces a sharp image. The choice of magnification? Your call. Many guides don't mind lugging around 10X50s and deal with the extra weight to get the high magnification and wide field of view that these powerful glasses provide. Others do just fine with the smaller and lighter 8X30s. The best advice is to find a quality pair at the magnification you want . . . and ones that you won't mind carrying around for twelve hours.

Speaking of carrying binoculars around—most hunters and every guide I have met in recent years immediately swap the factory-supplied strap for one that is wider and padded like those manufactured by Optec. In recent years, binocular harnesses like Butler Creek's Bino Buddy and Cabela's BinoSystem have become quite popular. These systems put the weight of the glasses over your shoulders instead of on your neck and keep them snug against your chest instead of swinging around.

Another category of optics is spotting scopes. Some hunters and guides use them regularly, and others don't use them at all. Many of California's pig areas are open enough to see targets at long distances. Spotting scopes are pressed into service when an animal needs to be sized up. This is particularly important if you are seeking a trophy boar. A spotting scope can give you a much more intimate look than you'd get otherwise. Variable-power spotting scopes are popular, with 20–60X models among the most frequently used. Don't forget a tripod or window mount to keep the scope stable.

In recent years, rangefinders have come down in price and have become a popular big-game hunting accessory. Many guides carry

This hunter has moved within 100 yards of a group of feeding hogs and is about to shoot. Once in shooting position, he will need to use a rest—dead tree, rock, or other support—to steady the shot.

one to take the guesswork out of their clients' shots, particularly the long ones. Nikon and Leica make quality rangefinders that pinpoint distances out to 800 yards, Bushnell makes medium-price models, and Ranging produces economy models for bow hunters (10 to 75 yards) and rifle hunters (50 to 1,000 yards).

Riflemen know well that a steady rest is vital to hitting the target. Bench shooters go to extremes to steady their rifles, and most hunters look for a rest as well. A rock or a tree will do, but often a makeshift rest just isn't available when you need to make a long shot. In recent years, bipods and shooting sticks have found great favor with hunters. I use a bipod made by Tony Diebold; other good ones include Harris bipods and Steady Stix.

If you are hunting without a guide, consider the following items before heading into the field. The first is a good knife to clean and eventually skin the animal. Quality knife makers including Buck, Gerber, and Schrade make everything from lock-blade folding models to straight-handle sheath knives. Blades four to six inches long are the most hunter-friendly. And don't forget the sharpener—few knives make it all the way through a cleaning and skinning job without getting dull. Several hunters and guides I know also bring disposable-blade utility knives, particularly for skinning. You'll need a bone saw to split a pig's pelvis and chest cavity, which is wise if you plan on hanging the animal for any length of time.

A good daypack will tote your food and extra clothing, along with rope, saws, and other gear. And if you're hunting without a guide, a packframe is essential. Get one with padded shoulder straps and a good hip belt. It's amazing how much weight can be hauled out with a good packframe. I've seen hogs lashed to one and packed out whole or, in the case of large animals, quartered. More details about this topic appear in a later chapter.

Some hunters prefer to drag animals out with a harness that distributes the weight of the hog over both of the dragger's shoulders. Cabela's sells a Deer Drag made of strong webbing and quarter-inch braided nylon rope for about $5. This method is far superior to dragging a pig out by its feet. If you must drag a hog out, a set of hay hooks placed behind the front or back hocks provide a handle and make the task easier. Other hunters use wheeled carriers, which take a lot of the strain out of transporting game.

Some other handy items: More and more hunters and guides are using rubber or surgical gloves when cleaning animals—not only to keep their hands clean but to prevent bacteria from entering scratches or cuts they may not even know they have. Another useful article is rope, which serves a multitude of uses, and don't forget a small piece of string to attach the tag to the game animal. Matches in a waterproof case can save your life, and insect repellent wards off mosquitoes and ticks, including the ones that carry Lyme disease.

Each hunter should tote along at least one gallon of water per day when it's hot, less when the weather is cool. In California, and most of North America for that matter, even clear-running streams contain the *Giardia* bacteria that make water unsafe to drink except under emergency situations. It's wise to bring along a power bar and other quick-energy food like dry fruit—you never know when you'll be in the field longer than planned. Finally, don't forget a camera, even if it's one of the throwaway models, to document your success.

## Chapter 3

Hunting Methods

Hunters use six basic methods to take wild hogs in California. They include stand hunting, spot-and-stalk, still hunting, drives, hunting with dogs, and tracking and calling. No matter what system you use, your first challenge will be checking for sign to substantiate that wild pigs are indeed using your hunting area. Signs to look for include well-used trails, tracks, droppings, mud wallows, bits of coarse hair on barbed-wire fences, rubs and tusk marks on trees, and the most telling sign of all—rooting. A heavily rooted area looks as if someone had run a rototiller through it. I've seen places where several hundred square feet of soft earth had been rooted up in a single night.

Wild hogs recently rooted up this area, which is a positive sign that hogs are using the area. Rooting often looks as if someone has just run a rototiller through the area.

No matter what hunting method is used, be on the lookout for sign to substantiate wild pigs are in your hunting area. This well-used trail leading from dense cover to an open feeding area is a good sign.

This hair was left by a wild hog when it crossed under the fence. Signs to look for include rooting, well-used trails, tracks, droppings, mud wallows, bits of coarse hair on a barbed-wire fence, and rubs or tusk marks on trees.

Find abundant fresh sign like that, and it's only a matter of time until you find the critters that left it!

Stand Hunting

Stand hunting is familiar to most hunters, whether they pursue white-tailed deer in Missouri, pronghorns in Wyoming, or elk in Colorado. Essentially, stand hunting is sitting in one location and waiting for the game to come to you. Whitetail hunters have elevated this concept to a near art form. More whitetails are killed from tree stands than by any other method. For western big game like pronghorn and desert mule deer, a good percentage of stand hunters use ground blinds near water holes.

Wild-pig hunters in California utilize the full range of stand techniques. Some areas are wooded enough to make a tree stand feasible. The secret is to scout the country thoroughly, looking for well-used trails. Where hogs are plentiful, main trails are used daily. Some lead from heavy-cover bedding areas to water; others go to and from feeding areas. In most cases, pigs will feed early in the day

Wild hogs like to rub the mud off their bodies on trees like this one. This is just another positive sign hogs are using an area.

If you can locate a watering area along a creek, at the edge of a lake, or near a stock pond, try to intercept pigs at the water source or as they travel to and from water. This method is especially effective during the hot summer months. Look for tracks around well-used water holes like this one; this shows that pigs are using the area.

and again late in the afternoon, returning to favored bedding areas during midday and at night. Hunters who find main trails and sit near them are often successful in ambushing pigs.

In addition to stands on well-used trails, setting up to intercept pigs at a water source or as they travel to and from it can be effective. One of my largest-ever wild boars was killed in August at the edge of a small stock pond near Paso Robles. The ranch owner told me that at least a dozen hogs had been watering there daily. I checked out the edge of the pond and found it covered with fresh pig tracks. I made a ground blind using dead tree limbs from an oak about seventy-five yards from the pond. I was in the blind before sunrise. At 8 A.M., a couple of deer and a few birds came to drink, but no hogs. I was about to give up when a group of fifteen pigs came out of the brush on the far side of the pond. They hesitated there for a moment, then trotted across a grassy field toward the water. When they stopped about fifteen yards from the pond and sniffed the air, I put my scope on a 275-pound boar, found the shoulder, and squeezed off a round. The boar whirled away at the impact of the bullet, but ran only fifty yards before it went down.

There's no question more pigs are killed in California by spot-and-stalk hunting than by all other methods combined. Someone once said spot-and-stalk hunting is 90 percent spot and 10 percent stalk. Be patient and spend plenty of time looking for your quarry.

The best time to hunt near water is during the hot and dry months from May to September. Once the rains come in the fall, the tuskers' use of water sources like stock ponds is less predictable. For a morning hunt, make sure you are set up before first light; in the afternoon, be in your stand at least an hour before the pigs start moving. Be quiet, don't smoke or eat, and make sure you relieve yourself before getting to the stand. Consider using a cover scent, particularly if you are a bow hunter using a ground blind. Try to place the stand so you are downwind of where the hogs are likely to approach your location. Make sure the stand offers clear shooting lanes, and know the approximate distances to the most probable target locations, particularly if you are using a bow or black powder.

Spot-and-Stalk Hunting

More pigs are killed in California by spot-and-stalk hunting than any other method—and maybe all other methods combined. Throughout most of the state's primary wild-hog habitat—the central

and north coast ranges as well as the foothills of the Sierra Nevada—
the terrain is a mixture of meadows, oak savanna, evergreen forest,
brush thickets, and riparian habitat. These areas are well suited to
spot-and-stalk hunting, the basic element of which is glassing open
and semi-open areas for hogs. This often takes plenty of patience
and can be tough on your eyes, so it is best accomplished with good-
quality optics. If you hunt hogs or other big game regularly, you will
spend hours using binoculars. Spotting scopes are used as well, to
size up animals after they are initially spotted with binoculars.

As mentioned above, wild hogs typically move from heavy cover
to feed early in the morning and again in the late afternoon or evening.
When it's rainy and/or overcast, however, they often feed all day
long. Favored feeding areas are the edges of heavy cover and open
fields. Along the central coast, for example, hogs frequent the barley
fields from the time the grain starts to form in May until the fields
are harvested in the fall. Hunters with access to such areas often set
up on a high point adjacent to the barley fields and wait for the hogs
to come out of the brush to feed.

At Dye Creek Preserve in Tehama County, spot-and-stalk accounts
for virtually 100 percent of the pigs killed. The hogs come out of the
heavy brush in the dark, feed all night, and stay out in the open for
the first hour or so of the day. If the weather is cool, they may stay
out longer, and if it's hot, they may go to water before returning to
the shady brush to wait out the midday heat. The guides on Dye
Creek have a dozen or more locations where they set up each morning
to glass for hogs. According to Dye Creek guide Jim Settle, the secret
is to glass, glass, and glass some more. Even though a group of hogs
may be using an area consistently, it doesn't necessarily mean they'll
be found there the next day. Daily movements are determined by
food, water, weather patterns, disturbance, predators, and breeding
chronology. At some point, however, they usually come out in the
open, and if you are in a position to spot and then initiate a stalk, you
will consistently harvest pigs. As with any other type of hunting,
look for movement or something out of the ordinary—a dark spot in
a field of dry yellow grass, a glint of light off a boar's tusk, a distant
cloud of dust, etc.

Once you spot a pig or group of them from a distance, plan the
stalk by taking into account the direction of the wind and the direction

the pigs are traveling. The time span from the initiation of the stalk to getting within range may be longer than you think, so try to get in front of the animals to intercept them and stay downwind to avoid being scented. Remember—their eyesight is poor, and you can sometimes get away with a sloppy approach, but a poorly planned and executed stalk that puts you upwind of your quarry generally spells disaster. When moving into position, it's always best to use cover as wisely as possible to avoid detection. I have belly-crawled across an open field, and as long as I moved slowly and stayed downwind of the pigs, I was able to get within fifty yards of the feeding animals. Once in shooting position, I almost always use a rest—a dead tree, rock, or bipod—and shoot from a sitting or kneeling position. In the absence of a good rest, take off your pack or roll up your jacket and use it to steady your rifle.

Still Hunting

In its purest form, still hunting is moving about an area, always on high alert for wild pigs. Often you'll detect a movement or sound, stop, assess the situation, then plan a stalk to get within shooting range. The key to still-hunting success is to move as quietly as possible. If hogs hear you first, they'll be gone before you get the opportunity for a shot. Equally important is moving slowly, stopping often to look and listen. Hogs are survivors and can pick up movement even if they cannot identify the moving object. Generally, they will bolt and run. Still hunting is almost always best accomplished alone. Two hunters, no matter how careful they are, make twice as much noise and give off twice as much scent as one hunter.

Once you spot hogs, you *must* position yourself downwind of the animals. If wild hogs smell you, they are gone—it's that simple! Do whatever it takes to get into position—belly-crawl, use cover, go around the animals. Sometimes it takes no more effort than just staying put. On several still-hunting occasions, I came upon a group of hogs in heavy cover less than sixty yards away. They didn't smell or see me, but because of the dense brush, not a single animal afforded a clear shot. If you wait long enough, hogs will eventually move, often toward you or at least into an opening for a clear shot. I've found that my chances of successfully waiting out a group of bedded hogs are best if I find them during midday and then wait for them to move out in the afternoon. Patience is definitely a virtue for a still hunter!

Drives

Though it takes several hunters to conduct a drive for wild pigs, it can be an effective method, particularly in areas too brushy for spot-and-stalk or where pig densities are not high enough to make stand hunting productive. It's also a good method to use during the middle of the day when the hogs are bedded down in heavy cover. Drives are still the preferred and most common method of hunting wild boar in Europe. The technique has reached its zenith in Germany and Eastern Europe, where dozens of beaters move the hogs through the woods to a line of waiting shooters. Once a hog is killed, it is strapped to a pole and hauled out of the woods. The kill is toasted with cognac and a great bonfire, and a hunting parade is followed by a meal to commemorate the hunt. Here in California, it's not quite so grand an affair—but it works!

Basically, the drivers move slowly through the brush, making a racket and hopefully moving the hogs toward the blockers, who stand fast at predetermined locations—often on well-used trails or other likely escape routes. The beaters can shoot pigs they jump up close, but they must be aware of the location of the other drivers and the blockers before they shoot. It's not unlike driving pheasants to the end of a cornfield—some pigs will double back and go around the beaters, others will run out the end without presenting a clean shot, and at times a group of pigs will come out all at once. But given some knowledge of the area and the general location the hogs have been using, driven hunts can put several pigs in the bag in short order.

Hunting with Dogs

According to CDF&G records, 10 to 15 percent of the successful hog hunters in California use dogs. A common method is to use a pack of trailing hounds that pick up the scent of a wild pig, then follow it until the hog decides to stop and hold its ground. The handler uses the barking of the dogs to keep track of their location. Other hunters use stock dogs, such as blue heelers and Border collies, that are relatively quiet until a pig is cornered. Then they let loose with a frenzy of barks, bays, and snarls—often mixed with pig squeals. At this point, hunters want to move in fast before a dog is injured. A cornered and angry 300-pound boar with good tusks can do a heap of damage to a dog. Virtually all pig hunters who use dogs will tell you they have lost one or more animals to an angry boar.

The sight of barking dogs surrounding and biting at a squealing, grunting, foaming-at-the-mouth, jaw-snapping boar will leave a lasting impression. Once the dogs corner a hog, the dog handler and hunters must move in quickly before the pig takes off again. According to Ken Whittaker, who guides on the north coast, it's best to move in quietly. A pig that is focused on the dogs rather than two or three hollering hunters might hold its ground a little longer and give you time to compose yourself and get off a shot. Pigs cornered by dogs are shot with rifles, bows, or pistols, usually at close range. Always be sure of your target and listen to your guide/dog handler—he'll tell you if a second shot is required or if it's time to climb a tree!

Certain areas in California allow the use of dogs all year for pig hunting; in other areas, dogs are restricted to specific times of year. Be sure to check current regulations.

Tracking and Calling

Though tracking is seldom used as a stand-alone technique for hogs, it is often one of the tools for spot-and-stalk or still hunting. Basically, hog tracks are located and the hunter follows them to the animal. In the East and Midwest where snowfall is common, tracking is more popular than it is here in California. However, the ability to track a hog, particularly over short distances, often means the difference between success and failure. Look for tracks that are blockier than those of deer, along with broken branches and strands of coarse hair left where pigs cross fence lines or pass through heavy brush.

Though not as widespread in California as it is in the Southeast, calling hogs is a tried-and-true method. I'm not talking about a down-on-the-farm hog-calling contest, but rather the use of pig squealers and hog grunters. Primos, Haydel, and Knight & Hale all make hog calls. Wild hogs are social creatures, and calling appeals to their curious nature and to their desire to find food and protect their young. Under the right circumstances, a seasoned caller can draw a wild boar out of thick brush in a matter of minutes. Calls can also be used to stop pigs that are ready to run away or have already spooked. Feeding calls are used to calm hogs that may have seen or heard you but are having difficulty figuring you out. If you can hold them for a few seconds, you just may get a shot.

Selecting the Animal

The majority of the hogs taken in California weigh one hundred to two hundred pounds on the hoof, putting them into the "meat-pig" category. Sow or boar, these are generally the best-eating animals. Though there is no legal restriction on the age or sex of wild pigs harvested in California, guides seldom allow a hog less than seventy-five or eighty pounds to be shot, and I don't know any who allow the taking of a sow with piglets. Piglets left to fend for themselves have a poor chance of survival—they are blue-plate specials to coyotes, bobcats, bears, and even big boars. Most wild-pig connoisseurs agree that a 125-pound barren sow is at the top of the list when it comes to table fare.

If you're after a trophy boar, there are several things to consider. The first is tusk length. Anything longer than two inches, measured from the gum line, is a trophy. Because the tusks are partly covered by the lips, they can be hard to evaluate. If you're with a guide, it's best to go with his assessment. If you're on your own, look for the tusks to be visible even at a hundred yards; if you can see an inch or more of exposed ivory, the tusk will likely make two inches total. If you have time, take a close look and make sure the boar has both tusks. Some boars break one tusk off, and you can be fooled by looking at only one side.

Here are a couple of other factors to consider in a potential trophy: Most hunters like a black boar. A true European boar is black, with a few brown or reddish hairs across the face and down the back. For many hunters, the closer a hog resembles its European ancestors, the more desirable it is for mounting. Additionally, scars on the face or

The majority of the wild pigs taken in California fall into the meat-pig category and weigh from 100 to 200 pounds, live weight. These are generally the best-eating animals, whether the animal be a sow or boar. This sow is a typical example of a nice meat hog.

The author took this nice meat hog on a northern California ranch. (Photo by Ben Myhre)

Most people define a trophy boar as an animal with tusks that measure two inches or more from the gum line. Look for the tusks to be visible even at 100 yards, and if you can see one or more inches of exposed ivory, then the tusk will likely make two inches total. A boar with tusks three inches or longer is rare and will fall into the upper 5 percent of the wild boars taken annually in California.

Pat Fisher's trophy boar had tusks that were nearly three inches in length and was taken with a compound bow. A boar with tusks more than two inches long is a trophy and stands a good chance of making it to the taxidermist.

tattered ears lend character to the mount of an old grizzled hog. In the final analysis, however, you are the one who determines whether a wild hog is a trophy or not!

Shot Placement

As with any big animal, the best place to hit a hog is in the vital organs, and the best way to do that on a broadside animal is to aim just behind the shoulder close to the upper leg bone. A shot in this general area will enter the lung cavity or hit the heart and put even a big boar down. A shot too far back will hit the liver or guts, and the animal will likely travel a long distance before going down.

Wild boars have a thick cartilaginous shield that covers the shoulder region. This band, often an inch or more thick, prevents boars from seriously harming each other during fights, which always involve slashing movements with their tusks. Boars are notorious for fighting over females, over food, and for any other reason that enters their tiny brains! Virtually all mature boars carry scars or open wounds from fighting.

The shoulder or immediately behind the shoulder close to the leg bone is the best place to aim. A shot in either of these areas will enter the lung cavity or hit the heart and put the animal down.

Most centerfire rifle cartridges will penetrate the thick layer of cartilage, but I have seen smaller-caliber bullets lodge in the cartilage or barely pass through it. I recently shot a hog in the shoulder, and the bullet—a 130-grain .270—entered the hog through the shield. The entry wound closed after impact, and the bullet did not exit the other side. Even close examination failed to reveal a hole in the animal. Chuck Harrison, who has done his share of hog hunting and guiding in Northern California, skinned a boar that had three .22 slugs either just under the skin or lodged as far as an inch deep in the cartilage. Nonetheless, a substantial bullet placed at or just behind the shoulder that penetrates this thick cartilaginous layer virtually guarantees a heart/lung shot and a clean kill.

Sows and young boars lack that thick protection found in older boars, but it's still best to aim at the shoulder. Head and neck shots are deadly but should be attempted only at relatively close range and by experienced shooters. These targets are small, and there is a high margin for error. Further, if you want to have a boar's head mounted, you do not want the damage a head shot causes. It is virtually impossible to mount a head-shot animal. Head and neck shots are not recommended in most pig-hunting scenarios. In all shooting situations, even if it's not a broadside shot, make sure your point of aim is a vital organ; otherwise, you risk losing the animal.

Because hogs have stubby legs, they appear shorter than they really are. Their low-slung profile often causes hunters to shoot high. Be aware of this, and when you obtain your sight picture, make sure the cross hairs center on the pig's midsection, not the top of its back. An exception would be a long shot where you must compensate for bullet drop.

Following Wounded Animals

Wild hogs are tough customers and are infamous for being able to take a solid hit and keep on going. Hogs shot in the heart or lungs, however, seldom run more than a hundred yards before keeling over, and pigs hit in the head, neck, or spine drop in their tracks. Hit one too far forward or too far back, and it may seem to go forever. Wounds in a hog's thick hide can close up on their own, leaving you a weak blood trail to follow. Start where you last saw the animal, and try to find where the first blood hit the ground or vegetation. Once you find blood, search intently for the next drop or smear and stay with it, looking for other signs, too—matted grass where the hog stopped to rest, broken twigs, overturned rocks, and the like. If you do approach a wounded hog, dispatch it as soon as you can, and aim for the vital organs. A wounded or cornered boar will come at you with fire in its eyes, hell-bent on inflicting serious damage with its tusks. Do it right—a trip to the hospital will likely ruin your day!

Approach even a "dead" hog with caution, keeping your weapon ready until you know it's finished. There is more than one story of a hunter walking up to a supposedly defunct hog, only to have it stand up and run away or, worse, turn to attack the hunter.

Chapter 4

Where to Hunt Wild Hogs

Between 1992 and 2000, California had an annual average of 33,300 wild-pig hunters. In 2000, a total of 42,705 pig tags were sold, including 40,963 resident and 1,742 nonresident tags. During the same time period, an average of 30,540 wild hogs were harvested annually. The 1997 harvest of 17,479 was the lowest, while the very next year's harvest of 52,516 was the highest. The 1998 figure was one of the highest kills on record, and '98 was the first year the state's pig harvest was greater than its deer kill. (Note harvest graph.)

Historically, wild-hog densities, the number of hogs harvested per square mile, and hunting success have gone hand in hand. It's simple—where there are lots of wild pigs, harvest and hunter success is high. So where are the areas of highest pig density? Most are along the coast range from Mendocino County to San Luis Obispo County, an area that

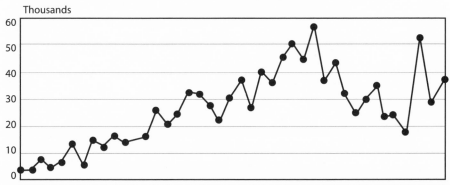

Reported Wild Pig Harvest (1960 - 2000)
From California Department of Fish and Game Hunter Survey

during the 1999–2000 license year (July 1 to June 30) produced 63 percent of the state's hog harvest. A distant second was the Southern Sierra/San Joaquin Valley region, where 18.3 percent of the harvest was recorded. The top ten counties in 2000 (the last year for which final figures are available at this writing) in descending order were Monterey, San Luis Obispo, Kern, San Benito, Santa Clara, Tehama, Sonoma, Santa Barbara, Fresno, and Mendocino. Monterey County has been the leader for years, with up to three times as many hogs harvested as in the Number 2 county, which rotates among San Luis Obispo, San Benito, and Santa Clara.

Even though slightly more than half of the land in California is privately owned, hog-harvest data indicates that about 90 percent are killed on private land. The balance are taken on public lands ranging from national forests and lands administered by the U.S. Bureau of Land Management (BLM) to military installations like Fort Hunter Liggett and Camp Roberts and State Wildlife Areas including Lake Sonoma and Tehama.

Wherever you hunt, it is important that you know exactly where you are, to avoid trespass problems. Maps of public areas

Geographically the areas of highest pig density are located in the coastal range from Mendocino County to San Luis Obispo County where during the 1999/2000 license year, 63 percent of the wild-hog harvest occurred. Here a hunter surveys wild-hog habitat in Mendocino County.

are available (some free, others for a small fee) from the agency that administers the land. For maps of federal land, contact U.S. Forest Service, 1323 Club Dr., Vallejo, CA 94592; 707-562-8737, or U.S. Bureau of Land Management, 2800 Cottage Way, Suite W1834, Sacramento, CA 95825; 916-978-4400.

Topographic maps are available from the U.S. Geological Survey's Distribution Center, Denver Federal Center, Building 810, Box 25286, Denver, CO 80225; 303-202-4700. Another source of excellent maps is the DeLorme Publishing Company, 2 DeLorme Dr., Yarmouth, ME 04096; 207-846-7000; Web site: www.delorme.com. DeLorme maps are available for California in two groupings—the Northern California Atlas and Gazetteer and the Southern California Atlas and Gazetteer.

The information provided in this chapter is current as of April 2002.

Open-Access Public Hunting Areas

These areas generally do not require an entry permit or fee and are open to hog hunting with the possession of a valid hunting license and pig tags. Be sure to observe any posted closures. Even though only 10 percent of the pigs bagged in California come from public land, there are vast opportunities to hunt them on lands administered primarily by the U.S. Forest Service (USFS) and BLM. While these hunts are economical and can be accomplished with little more than good boot leather and a rifle, there is no question that hog hunting on open-access public land is difficult. The terrain is generally steep and brushy, and access can be difficult—some of the better hunting is in wilderness areas where vehicles are prohibited. Using dogs can increase your chances for success, but hog densities are generally low on most public land, and you'll see fewer hogs there than on private land or on controlled-access public areas. Hunter success is often as low as 1 or 2 percent; rarely is it 10 percent. Because of the difficulties involved, however, you will see very few other hog hunters. A freelance expedition on public land is possible if you do your homework and are willing to spend time in the field. A boar taken on public land in a classic fair-chase setting is a well-earned trophy that you will remember forever.

U.S. Bureau of Land Management—Arcata Field Office
1695 Heindon Rd., Arcata, CA 95521
707-825-2300
Web site: www.ca.blm.gov/arcata

BLM's Arcata office administers about 185,000 acres of federal lands in Humboldt, Trinity, and Mendocino counties. Hog sightings have been reported throughout the field-office area, but there are two specific locations where hogs are known to exist. The largest is the 56,000-acre King Range National Conservation Area in Humboldt County, southwest of Garberville. Even here, the pigs move on and off the public land from adjacent private holdings, and densities are low. It takes plenty of effort to find and kill hogs here.

Two areas within the King Range give hunters the best probability of seeing pigs. The first is Bear Trap Ridge, accessed via the Smith-Etter Road about 1½ miles south of the Honeydew Store. The area is mostly tan oak and madrone thickets interspersed with oak woodland and coastal prairie. Douglas fir dominates the northern slopes and better soils. The other location is Paradise Ridge in the southern portion of the King Range. It is accessible via the Shelter Cove Road to the Paradise Ridge Road, which goes north about four miles. The habitat is a mixture of annual grassland, hardwood forest, and brushlands. Both areas share a common border with private land, and care should be taken to avoid trespassing. There are several campgrounds in the area, and a map of the King Range is available from the Arcata Field Office for $4.

In addition to the King Range, hogs can be found in the Elkhorn Ridge portion of the South Fork Eel River Management Area. Here about 5,500 acres of public land straddles the South Fork of the Eel River. From Laytonville, take Branscomb Road about 2½ miles to Wilderness Lodge Road. Stay on the west side of the river and follow the road to the top of Elkhorn Ridge. The habitat is tan oak and madrone forest with a few grassy openings. Private holdings are mixed in with the public land, so be sure you know where you are hunting. Pigs are widely scattered, and the country is so steep and rough it might be a good place to send someone you want to punish!

Bureau of Land Management—Folsom Field Office
63 Natoma St., Folsom, CA 95630
916-985-4474
Web site: www.ca.blm.gov/folsom

The Folsom office oversees about 250,000 acres in the Central Valley and Sierra Foothills. Only one location is known to support wild pigs. The Hunter Valley Recreation Area covers about 10,000 acres of foothill country, mostly south and east of Coulterville in Mariposa County. The habitat is chaparral brushland with some annual grassland and limited oak woodlands. About 80 percent of the area burned in an August 2000 wildfire that nearly obliterated the habitat. However, as often occurs after a fire, dense brush was replaced by tender new vegetation, and wildlife populations generally responded favorably. Look for improved habitat conditions and expanding hog populations in the future. Currently, pig densities are low and the animals are widely scattered. Access is via Highway 49 to Bear Valley Road to Hunter Valley Road.

Bureau of Land Management—Hollister Field Office
20 Hamilton Ct., Hollister, CA 95023
831-630-5000 or the 24-hour information number (831-630-5050)
Web site: www.ca.blm.gov/hollister

The Hollister office, in the central coast range, covers 385,000 acres in scattered parcels from San Francisco Bay to the San Luis Obispo County line and from the Pacific Ocean to Interstate 5. Due to the scattered nature of the BLM land, hunters should contact the Hollister office and purchase a packet of ownership maps ($4) so they do not stray onto private lands. This packet can be obtained in person at the office or by sending a check or money order payable to USDI-BLM to the Hollister Field Office at the address above.

Wild hogs inhabit the entire area, but sporadically and at low densities. Four areas provide the best bets for pig hunters. Laguna Mountain, a 10,000-acre block in southern San Benito County, is a mixture of chaparral and oak grassland. The hogs trade back and forth between private grain fields, where they feed, and the public land, where dense brush provides shelter. The area is closed to vehicles; access is by foot, horseback, or mountain bike. There are three access points off the Coalinga/Las Gatos Creek Road.

The 50,000-acre Clear Creek Management Area, also in southern San Benito County, is open to vehicles, and offroad use is permitted on more than 270 miles of dirt trails that traverse the area. The management area includes 5,241-foot Mt. San Benito, tallest peak in the Diablo Range. Much of the area supports chaparral, which is of low value to wildlife. However, there are pockets of live oak and grassland, and pines dominate the higher elevations. The oak/pine areas support the best pig populations.

It should be pointed out that portions of the Clear Creek Management Area have naturally occurring asbestos particles in the soil. If you suffer from respiratory problems, this may be a place you want to avoid, particularly when the wind blows. Safety precautions are available from the BLM. Information on current road conditions and dust levels is available via the 24-hour Clear Creek Conditions hotline (831-630-5060). Most of the asbestos deposits are found in the dense chaparral areas, which are generally poor hog habitats.

The Stockdale Mountain area in Monterey County is a 3,000-acre block that is almost entirely dense chaparral. The hogs feed on adjacent private land, then move to the brush on BLM land for cover. Hunters must be careful not to trespass on private land and stay in areas open to hunting. The area is accessible from Highway 101 at San Miguel via the Vineyard Canyon Road to the Slacks Canyon Road, or from Interstate 5 and Parkfield to the Vineyard Canyon Road.

Finally, there are a few hogs in the Coalinga Mineral Springs area in Fresno County. Here yucca and saltbush dominate the dry south slopes, and manzanita, scrub oak, and scattered gray pine are the primary vegetation on the north slopes. Hogs trade between the public area and adjacent private lands and are difficult to locate. Access is off Highway 198 southwest of Coalinga, via the Coalinga Mineral Springs Road. Camping is available at the Coalinga Mineral Springs Park, operated by Fresno County.

My daughter's first big-game animal was a nice meat pig. Here she is with a trophy boar.

Bureau of Land Management—Redding Field Office
355 Hemsted Dr., Redding, CA 96002
530-224-2100
Web site: www.ca.blm.gov/redding

Within the 250,000 acres administered by the Redding office, one area is known to support hogs. The Sacramento Bend Area covers about 17,000 acres and stretches from Battle Creek on the north to Highway 36 on the south, west to the Sacramento River and east one to four miles. The eastern boundary is the most difficult to determine and abuts private land. A free *User Guide to the Sacramento River* is available from the Redding office. The area is in Tehama County just south of the Shasta County line.

Pigs have long been present in the lower Inks Creek and Paynes Creek drainage areas, but all were on private land. With BLM's acquisition of the Sacramento Bend Area, beginning in the early 1970s, some of these lands became public domain and open to hunting. By the early 1990s, a substantial amount of acreage had been acquired and pig hunters discovered this new area. Pig densities are low, but thanks to good habitat, their numbers are stable. Hunting remains a challenge because of the heavy vegetation, particularly along the Sacramento River and its tributaries, and because the hogs move off the area to private holdings, where they are hunted regularly.

The area is a combination of riverine forest along the Sacramento and blue-oak woodland and annual grasslands as you move away from the river. The western section is accessible by boat from the Sacramento River. Access to the central and southern portions is via Interstate 5 to Jelly's Ferry Road and then Bend Ferry Road. The southeastern section can be reached off Highway 36 east of Red Bluff. The northern portion is accessible via Interstate 5 at Anderson to Balls Ferry Road, then Gover Road, then Spring Branch Road.

Bureau of Land Management—Ukiah Field Office
2550 N. State St., Ukiah, CA 95482
707-468-4000
Web site: www.ca.blm.gov/ukiah

The Ukiah office administers about 300,000 acres of land in Mendocino, Lake, Colusa, and Yolo counties. Though this is federal land, some areas are landlocked (completely surrounded by private land), making access difficult to impossible, while others are in large blocks where access is good. The most stable pig populations are found in the Cache Creek drainage, about twenty-five miles southwest of Williams and eight miles east of Clearlake Oaks. Currently, the Cache Creek Natural Area is 73,500 acres. Prior to 1985, however, the area totaled 53,000 acres, and much of it was landlocked due to inadequate public access. In 1985, 20,000 acres were added, and in 1987, CDF&G purchased a key parcel adjacent to State Highway 20, making access to the full acreage possible. The area is managed cooperatively by BLM and CDF&G.

About two-thirds of the Cache Creek Natural Area is dense chamise brushland; the remainder is a mix of oak woodlands, annual grasslands, and riparian habitat along Cache Creek. The natural area is closed to vehicles and accessible only by foot, horseback, and mountain bike. More and more hunters are discovering that in areas where vehicles are restricted, mountain bikes are an excellent method of transportation.

There are two main access points to the natural area. The North Fork parking area is located on the south side of Highway 20, eight miles east of Clearlake Oaks and thirty miles west of Williams. This is the trailhead for the Redbud Trail. The Judge Davis Trailhead parking area is approximately eight miles to the east, also on Highway 20. In the near future, additional access points will likely be established on Highway 16, providing access to the most recent land acquisitions. Most of the natural area is in Lake County, with smaller portions in Colusa and Yolo counties.

The use of dogs for hunting wild pigs is not permitted on the CDF&G portion of the natural area (Cache Creek Wildlife Area, approximately 2,600 acres). Dogs can be used on the balance of the area from the beginning of deer season until the first Saturday in April.

The Indian Valley Reservoir/Walker Ridge area, about twenty-five miles west of Williams, also harbors wild pigs. They move between BLM land and USFS land on the Mendocino National Forest. The area is located on the Colusa/Lake County line, and access is off Highway 20. It is steep, brushy country that is hot in summer and can get muddy and difficult to access in the winter. Vehicles are permitted on designated roadways only. There are about 40,000 acres of BLM land and 5,000 acres of CDF&G land (Indian Valley Wildlife Area) that support low-density hog populations. Dogs can be used from the beginning of deer season until the first Saturday in April.

A third unit overseen by the Ukiah BLM office is the 50,000-acre Cow Mountain Recreation Area between Ukiah and Clear Lake in Lake and Mendocino counties. The recreation area is mostly chamise/chaparral brushland, with some oaks and grass on the north slopes. The area is steep, and hunting is difficult. There are two units—South Cow Mountain (23,000 acres) and North Cow Mountain (27,000 acres). The south unit is a designated offroad-vehicle (ORV) area with more than 125 miles of roads. ORV use can be heavy, and the habitat here does not support many hogs. Most pig hunting is done in the north unit, especially in the riparian areas and drainages on the west slope of Cow Mountain, particularly those with flowing water. Dogs can be used here all year. Access is off Highway 101 east of Ukiah to Talmage Road (east), south on East Side Road, then east on Mill Creek Road to the Mill Creek County Park. Just past the park, go left to North Cow Mountain or straight to South Cow Mountain.

California Dept. of Forestry—Jackson Demonstration State Forest
802 North Main St., Fort Bragg, CA 95437
707-964-5674

This "demonstration forest" covers about 50,000 acres along Highway 20 between Willits and Fort Bragg in Mendocino County. Administered by the California Department of Forestry and Fire Protection, it is a mix of dense conifer forests and hardwood/conifer woodlands. The west and central portions are ten- to one-hundred-year-old stands of redwoods and Douglas fir while the eastern section supports brush and conifer/hardwood habitats dominated by tan oak, redwood, and Douglas fir. Pigs are hard to find here, thanks to dense vegetation, limited visibility, and low populations. However, those willing to tough it out might try the North Fork of the Big River and its tributaries, accessible via roads in the Camp 20 vicinity along Highway 20. There are several camping areas, offroad travel is not permitted, and the area is subject to seasonal road closures. Maps are available.

U.S. Army Corps of Engineers—Pine Flat Reservoir
P.O. Box 117, Piedra, CA 93649
559-787-2589

The Army Corps of Engineers (COE) administers about 13,000 acres of grassland and brush at Pine Flat Reservoir in Fresno County. The area available for hunting varies from a few hundred to a few thousand acres, depending on the lake level. However, only a few hundred acres (at full pool) on the south side of the lake support hogs. The south side is a combination of public land (Sequoia National Forest), COE land, and private holdings. The narrow band of COE land around the lake serves more as an access corridor to USFS holdings than as a hunting area. The only access to the south shore is by boat. There are launch ramps at Deer Creek, Island Park, Lake View, and Trimmer, all on the north shore, accessible from Highway 99 via Belmont Avenue to Trimmer Springs Road.

Hog populations are low and vary seasonally. A few pigs use the reservoir as their primary water source during the summer months. Hunting is permitted yearlong, and only shotguns are legal. A map and specific hunting regulations are available.

U.S. Forest Service—Los Padres National Forest
6755 Hollister Ave., Suite 150, Goleta, CA 93117
805-968-6640
Web site: www.r5.fs.fed.us/lospadres

Most people familiar with pig hunting on California's public lands agree that the single best open-access opportunity is on the Los Padres National Forest, a 1.75-million-acre chunk of land in Monterey, San Luis Obispo, Santa Barbara, Ventura, Los Angeles, and Kern counties. It is wide open to hunting (except for a few designated no-firearm zones) and supports a decent population of wild pigs. The terrain varies from oak savanna to dense chaparral and conifer forest and almost everything in between.

Some of the better pig densities are found in the Santa Lucia Range in Monterey County and the San Rafael Mountains in Santa Barbara County (particularly east of Lake Cachuma). In the Monterey Ranger District (831-385-5434), the Ventana Wilderness is known for producing large boars that are a mix of feral hogs and true European wild boar. The San Rafael Wilderness in the Santa Barbara (805-967-3481) and Santa Lucia (805-925-9538) ranger districts is another good hog area. In the wilderness areas, access is by foot or horseback and you'll have to haul in your drinking water and other supplies. The best way to hunt these areas is to set up a centrally located base camp and hunt out from there each day.

Even in areas with moderate hog densities, hunting on the Los Padres is tough, and you must be in good shape and spend serious time glassing and hiking to be successful. Wild pigs here have large home ranges—they can be in one area today and miles away the next day. They use certain areas seasonally, but not the same areas every year. When there is a good acorn crop, pigs will use the oak woodland and savanna areas extensively in the fall. If the acorn crop fails the next year, they may be completely absent from the same area. The hot summer months can be uncomfortable on the central coast, but pig hunting then can be productive because you can concentrate on water sources. Find a place where a group of hogs has been watering recently, and it's worth spending time there waiting for them to get thirsty. Otherwise, this country is best suited to a combination of careful still hunting and spot-and-stalk.

To reduce exposure of the endangered California condor and other scavengers on Los Padres to lead poisoning, the USFS, CDF&G, and the U.S. Fish and Wildlife Service request that hunters bury gut piles to a depth and in a location that will discourage scavengers. Additionally, they suggest using bullets that do not leave lead residues in game. Cartridges loaded with X-Bullets (PMC Gold, El Dorado, and some Federal Premium ammo) or Fail Safe Bullets (some Winchester Supreme) do not leave a lead residue.

To participate in any form of recreation on the Los Padres National Forest, an Adventure Pass is required. It costs $5 a day or $30 a year and can be obtained from any of the national forest offices and local vendors. All visitors must display the pass in their vehicle when they park on the Los Padres.

U.S. Forest Service—Mendocino National Forest
825 N. Humboldt Ave., Willows, CA 95988
530-934-3316
Web site: www.r5.fs.fed.us/mendocino

Three areas within the 886,000-acre Mendocino National Forest support low- to moderate-density pig populations. The first is the Indian Valley Reservoir area west of Maxwell. Access is off Highway 20 via Walker Ridge Road or the Sites/Maxwell Road (Oak Street) due west of Maxwell. Much of the area adjoins land administered by BLM's Ukiah office, and the hogs regularly move between USFS, BLM, and private land. The habitat is largely chamise brush with open grasslands and scattered oaks. The USFS portion covers about 10,000 acres in the Grindstone (530-934-3316) and Upper Lake (707-275-2361) ranger districts.

The second area is the Grindstone Creek region in the Grindstone Ranger District. Wild pigs inhabit about 15,000 acres of chamise brushlands, scattered woodlands, and riparian habitat in Glenn County. The area can be reached off Highway 162 and Forest Service Road M9 near Elk Creek.

Finally, the Jump Off Creek Drainage and the Etsel Ridge area in Mendocino County also have wild hogs. They roam over about 25,000 acres east of Covelo on the northwest edge of the Mendocino Forest in the Covelo Ranger District (707-983-6118). The habitat ranges from open glades and oak woodland at lower elevations to pine and white fir at elevations of 5,000 to 6,000 feet. The area is ten to twelve miles east of Covelo off Highway 162 via Forest Service Roads M1 and FH7.

The best hunting here is during fall and winter, when the animals feed on acorns in the oak woodlands. Some hunters prefer the hot summer months, when the hogs are found near water. Hunting pressure can cause the pigs here to change their feeding routine from early and late in the day to a nocturnal pattern, making them much more difficult to hunt. The use of dogs will increase your chances. However, there is some controversy over using dogs: Spot-and-stalk hunters often claim they run the pigs out of the country. Hunter success is generally low, but if you do your homework and hunt hard, there are pigs to shoot on the Mendocino.

To reduce exposure from lead poisoning to the endangered California condor on the Los Padres National Forest, the U.S. Fish and Wildlife Service, California Department of Fish and Game, and the U.S. Forest Service request that hunters bury gut piles to discourage scavengers. Additionally, they suggest using bullets that do not leave lead residues when penetrating game.

U.S. Forest Service—Sequoia National Forest
900 West Grand Avenue, Porterville, CA 93257
559-784-1500
Web site: www.r5.fs.fed.us/sequoia

Two areas within the 1.1-million-acre Sequoia National Forest support wild pigs. One is the Hume Lake Ranger District (559-338-2251) in Fresno County, about 8,000 acres of mostly chaparral and blue-oak woodland. It encompasses Oat Mountain, Pine Ridge, and Camp 4½ and extends roughly from the Forest boundary on the west to Davis Flat Road (Forest Service Road 12SO1) on the east, south to Highway 180, and north to the Kings River and Pine Flat Reservoir. The better areas here are those least accessible. Road access is from Highway 180 and Davis Flat Road. Some hunters use boats to reach the south shore of Pine Flat Reservoir, where they can access COE and USFS land. There are launch ramps at Deer Creek, Island Park, Lake View, and Trimmer, all on the north shore. The area is steep, the brush thick, and hunting difficult, but pigs are present all year.

The Sequoia's second pig area is in the Greenhorn Ranger District (760-379-5646) in Kern and Tulare counties. The pig region is about 4,000 acres and is dominated by chaparral, blue-oak woodland, and scattered riparian habitat along the drainage. It's only been since the mid-1990s that hogs have moved from private land onto public land in the Greenhorn District. That public land is roughly between McFarland Creek on the north and Alder Creek on the south, west to the Forest boundary, and east to elevations of 4,000 to 4,500 feet. To get there, take Highway 155 out of Glennville to Forest Service Roads 24SO7 and 25SO4. Hog populations are low but appear to be increasing, particularly in the more remote areas.

Other Public Areas

Wild pigs have been reported on a number of other public areas in California, generally only on a transient basis. In other words, a few might be present for a few days or weeks and then move off the area, and months may go by before another pig is sighted. Because the hunting here is unpredictable, I provide only contact information:

- U.S. Forest Service, Six Rivers National Forest, Mad River Ranger District, Star Route, Box 300, Bridgeville, CA 95526; 707-574-6233
- California Department of Fish and Game, Big Sandy Wildlife Area, Lower Ragsdale Dr., #100, Monterey, CA 93940; 831-649-2870
- California Department of Fish and Game, Little Panoche Reservoir Wildlife Area and San Luis Reservoir Wildlife Area, 18110 West Henry Miller Rd., Los Banos, CA 93635; 209-826-0463
- U.S. Forest Service, Stanislaus National Forest, Groveland Ranger District, 24545 Highway 120, Groveland, CA 95321; 209-962-7825
- California Department of Forestry and Fire Protection, Boggs Mountain State Forest, P.O. Box 839, Cobb, CA 95426; 707-928-4378
- California Department of Fish and Game, Putah Creek Wildlife Area, 1701 Nimbus Rd., Rancho Cordova, CA 95670; 916-358-2900
- U.S. Bureau of Land Management, Arcata Field Office, Red Mountain Recreation Area, 1695 Heindon Rd., Arcata, CA 95521; 707-825-2300
- U.S. Forest Service, Sierra National Forest, Kings River Ranger District, 29688 Auberry Rd., Prather, CA 93651; 559-855-5355
- Bureau of Land Management, Bakersfield Field Office, Squaw Leap Management Area, 3801 Pegasus Dr., Bakersfield, CA 93308; 661-391-6000.

Limited-Access Public Hunting Areas

These places are mostly on military bases, other federal lands, and CDF&G wildlife areas. Access is limited, and in many cases an entry fee is charged. Hog hunting is open only during certain times of the year, often only on specific days of the week, and hunter numbers are generally controlled by a lottery draw or entry is first-come, first-served until a quota is met. As on the open-access public areas, the hunting here is often difficult—steep terrain, dense brush, and low to moderate hog densities work against you. However, because hunter numbers are limited and some of the areas support moderate pig populations, success rates are a notch above the open-access areas, generally ranging from 5 to about 10 percent. An exception is the Joice Island Wildlife Area, where hunter success regularly tops 60 percent. Dogs are not permitted on the majority of the limited-access public areas.

CDF&G—Cottonwood Creek Wildlife Area
18110 West Henry Miller Rd., Los Banos, CA 93635
209-826-0463

This area in Merced County is made up of two units, Lower Cottonwood and Upper Cottonwood. Pig populations are low on both units, and hunter success runs 5 to 10 percent. Pigs can be hunted on both units from the start of the A-Zone archery deer season (mid-July) until the last Sunday in January. There is no entry fee, and camping is not permitted. The Lower Unit covers about 2,000 acres of rolling grassland along with a small riparian area and limited brushlands. Here weapons are restricted to bows and shotguns, except during the archery deer season when only bows can be used. Reservations are not required, and there is no hunter quota. The Lower Unit can be reached off Highway 152 about fifteen miles west of Los Banos; head to the San Luis Creek Recreation Area entrance, then to the parking area marked Cottonwood Creek Wildlife Area. Access from the parking area is on foot only.

The Upper Unit covers about 4,000 acres of oak woodland and chaparral along with scattered annual grasslands. The hunting period is the same, but any legal weapon, including centerfire rifles, can be used. There is no hunter quota, except that during the opening weekend of the A-Zone deer season a special permit issued by a lottery drawing is required. The Upper Unit is 20 miles west of Los Banos on Highway 152 (roughly between Pacheco Pass and where Highway 152 crosses San Luis Reservoir). From the parking area, access is on foot only.

CDF&G—Joice Island Wildlife Area
2548 Grizzly Island Rd., Suisun, CA 94585
707-425-3828

This 1,800-acre, state-operated area is one of the units administered by Grizzly Island Wildlife Area. Joice Island is largely wetlands: thick cattails and tules, some brush, and open-water ponds. Hogs seem to do just fine in this marshy environment. A public pig hunt has been conducted annually since 1998, with excellent results. Several large boars in the 250-pound range have been harvested, and hunter success has ranged from 50 to 80 percent, averaging about

60 percent. One result is that the number of applicants is high and the chances of drawing a permit are relatively low—about fifty to one. But if you get drawn, there's a high probability you'll bring home the bacon! The hunts are conducted only on selected weekend days between early February and late March. The first weekend is reserved for junior-license holders at least twelve years of age; the rest of the weekends are open to any licensed hunter who draws a permit. The hunts are one day in length, and only two hunters per day are allowed on Joice Island, for a total of four hunters per weekend. You apply by sending a standard postcard with your name, address, telephone number, hunting license number, and choice of a single weekend date to Joice Island Wild Pig Hunt at the address above. Each hunter can apply only once per season, but parties of two can apply on a single postcard. Applications are accepted between 1 December and mid-January. There is no entry fee, and only shotguns with slugs can be used.

CDF&G—Lake Sonoma Wildlife Area
P.O. Box 47, Yountville, CA 94599
707-944-5500

This area is a cooperative venture between the COE, which owns the land, and CDF&G, which manages the hunting programs. The 8,000-acre area is located off Highway 101, about eight miles west of Cloverdale. The up-and-down habitat is mostly oak savanna and chamise, but it's more open than many other limited-access hunting areas. The area holds a small resident population of pigs as well as a group that moves between adjacent private lands and the wildlife area. These movements tend to be seasonal, with the highest number of hogs present on the wildlife area during the winter months. In recent years, hunter success has ranged from 2 percent for archers to 13 percent for rifle hunters, averaging 5 percent for all hunting methods. The area is open during two hunting periods—early November to early January and mid-January to late March. Hunting is permitted every Tuesday and one or two Wednesdays per month during the open period. The Tuesday hunts are archery only during the first hunt period (fall) and shotguns with slugs during the second period (spring). The Wednesday hunts are reserved for rifle hunters during both periods.

The deadline for submitting applications for Period 1 hunts is early October, and for Period 2 it's mid-December. Hunters can apply by submitting a standard postcard to Lake Sonoma Wild Pig Hunt at the address above. You can apply for only one hunt date in each period. Two hunters can be listed on each card, which must carry their names, addresses, phone numbers, hunting license numbers, and choice of date. Fifteen permits per hunt day are issued by lottery, and there is no access fee.

CDF&G—Spenceville Wildlife Area
94520 Oro Dam Blvd. West, Oroville, CA 95965
530-538-2236

Spenceville is 11,400 acres in Nevada and Yuba counties, about ten miles east of Marysville as the crow flies, and it abuts the eastern boundary of Beale Air Force Base. The hogs move on and off Spenceville from adjacent private lands and the military base. The habitat is blue-oak woodland and annual grassland, with riparian areas along three intermittent streams, Little Dry, Dry, and Cox creeks. Access is good: Hamilton/ Smartsville Road bisects the area north to south, and Spenceville/Auburn Ravine Road bisects it in an east-to-west direction. Hunters park in designated areas and then hunt on foot.

The area is open daily from 1 September to 31 January, and there is no fee or hunter quota. This is one of the few limited-access public areas where dogs are permitted for pig hunting. Any legal weapon can be used. Success rates are low—5 percent or less—but for hunters who concentrate their efforts during September, particularly the first week or so after the area opens, rates are in the 10 to 15 percent range. The area can get crowded on 1 September, the opening of the dove season.

CDF&G—Tehama Wildlife Area
P.O. Box 188, Paynes Creek, CA 96075
530-597-2201

This 46,000-acre area, twenty-three miles east of Red Bluff, is a mixture of oak and foothill pine interspersed with grasslands and brush. Elevation ranges from 1,000 to more than 3,000 feet, and the area supports low- to moderate-density hog populations. The hogs move on and off the property, and if they're present when the hunt is being conducted, sightings and hunter success can be fair. If not, the hunt is a bust. Over the years, hunter success has ranged from 2 to 12 percent, averaging about 6 percent.

During February and March, hog hunting is permitted on eight consecutive weekends on 30,000 acres of the area. The hogs can be anywhere, but the southwest corner (Section 33), which borders the private Dye Creek Preserve, generally produces the best hunting. Twenty-five or thirty permits per weekend are awarded by a lottery draw; the deadline to submit applications is early January. The odds of drawing for opening weekend are about twenty-five to one; on the last weekend virtually every applicant gets a permit. However, very few hogs are killed the final weekend. There is no access fee. Rifles, shotguns, muzzleloaders, and archery equipment are all legal. Individual hunters or a group of up to four can apply by sending a standard postcard with names, addresses, telephone numbers, hunting license numbers, and specific dates to Tehama Wild Pig Hunt at the address above. You may submit only one application per year.

California National Guard—Camp Roberts
HQ Camp Roberts
ATTN: Hunting & Fishing Program
Camp Roberts, CA 93451
805-238-8167

Camp Roberts is a National Guard Training Base just north of Paso Robles. Its 43,000 acres support low to moderate hog densities and are a mixture of annual grasslands, oak woodlands, and riparian habitats. Hogs use the grasslands extensively in the spring, moving to the riparian areas in the summer and to the oak woodlands in the fall to feed on acorns. Some hogs stay on the area all year, but most periodically move off-base to adjacent private lands, particularly along the southern boundary, then back again. Hunts have been offered on Camp Roberts for years, and annual hunter success ranges up to 10 percent. The key to the hog habitat here (as in most areas) is rainfall. When precipitation is above average, vegetation proliferates and so do hog populations. Under drought conditions, the habitat and the pig population can suffer.

About 35,000 acres are open to hunters on selected days between late April and early January. However, military exercises frequently modify the schedule, so it is always best to call or write before planning a trip. The daily access fee is $15, an annual pass is $55, and the fees can be paid on site. Young people with a valid junior hunting license get in free. Entry is first-come, first-served until a quota of 250 big-game hunters is reached. To date, the quota has never been reached, except on opening weekend of the A-Zone rifle deer season (in August), which requires an advance reservation. All hunters must register at the check station at Gate 3 off Highway 101. Recreational vehicle parking with full hookups is available for $12 a day, and rooms can be reserved for $15.50 a day by calling Camp Roberts Billeting at 805-238-8312. For information, send a self-addressed, stamped envelope to the address above.

U.S. Air Force—Vandenberg Air Force Base
Game Warden, 30 SFS/SFOW
108 Colorado Blvd., Vandenberg AFB, CA 93437
805-606-6804

Vandenberg is located near Lompoc in Santa Barbara County and covers 99,100 acres. The base supports low-to-moderate hog populations and is a mixture of coastal sage scrub, oak woodland, chamise brushlands, and riparian habitats. Pig hunting is open every day all year, but there is a serious catch. Pig hunting is restricted to:

1) active military personnel and their dependents;
2) retired military personnel and their dependents;
3) military reservists from all branches;
4) Santa Inez Chumash Indian tribal members;
5) Department of Defense civilian employees attached to Vandenberg, not including contractors;
6) employees of the federal prison at Lompoc.

A hunter's chances are relatively good here, and 100 to 150 hogs are taken annually. In recent years, in some areas of the base, the hog population has increased to a point that hogs have been removed under depredation permits.

Authorized individuals must buy a Base Wild Pig Hunting Stamp ($15.50 for active or retired military, $35.50 for civilians) at the Base Exchange, then take it to the Fish and Wildlife Office, where you get a thirty-day base hunting permit. At times, the hunting area is closed due to military activities.

U.S. Army—Fort Hunter Liggett Military Reservation
Commander, Fort Hunter Liggett Military Reservation
P.O. Box 7091
Attn: AFRC-FMH-DPW-E
Fort Hunter Liggett, CA 93928
831-386-3310 (recorded message)
Web site: www.liggett.army.mil

This central-coast reservation is a 165,000-acre expanse of annual grassland, oak woodlands, and chaparral in southwestern Monterey County, about twenty-five miles southwest of King City via Jolon Road. It offers some of the better limited-access public hog hunting in California. The Reservation is so large that most of the hogs spend their entire lives within its confines. Compared to most other limited-access areas, hunters here have a greater opportunity to figure out where the hogs live and hunt them successfully. Still, the pigs range far and wide, and killing one requires effort.

The area is divided up into numbered training areas. Some are closed to hunting; some are walk-in only and restricted to shotguns, bows, and muzzleloaders (areas 29 and 30) or archery only (training area 3); most others have road access and are open to rifle hunters. Some of the better hog populations are in the southwestern quadrant, north of the hunter check station in training areas 10/13 and 30 and 29 adjacent to San Antonio Lake. Hog-hunting success here is impossible to determine, but every year 100 to 150 hogs are taken.

Up to 130,000 acres of Hunter Liggett are open most weekends and federal holidays, but the base can be closed due to military training operations. Before leaving home, hunters should always call the recorded information telephone number to ensure that hunting will be permitted that weekend.

The process of obtaining a permit is complicated and frankly something of a pain in the neck! The first step is to write, call, or check this Web site: www.liggett.army.mil. Click on "About the Garrison," go to "Hunting & Fishing," "Rules and Regulations" and look for a voucher request form. Once you get it, fill it out and return it along with $70 for an annual permit or $25 for a two-day permit. (The area has good small-game and deer hunting, and an annual permit allows multiple entries.) Only money orders are accepted; checks or any other form of payment will be returned, and the process will come to a grinding halt. In two to three weeks, you will receive in the mail a voucher that is redeemable for a hunting permit (the voucher is essentially a receipt indicating the entry fee has been paid). To get the actual hunting permit, present the voucher at the hunter-registration window located at the primitive campground. Access is first-come, first-served, and if all training areas are open to hunting (which is rare), up to 790 hunters can be accommodated. Other than during the opening weekend of rifle deer season, your chances of gaining access are good. You'll be assigned to a training area. You can change it by returning to the check station and inquiring if space is available in another area. You must check out after hunting and declare all game taken. Serious hog hunters should avoid the first weekend of deer season and the dove and quail opening weekends, when the reservation can get crowded.

Space in the primitive campground is available on a first-come, first-served basis; the $5 daily fee is payable via a drop box on site. The campground has limited water and toilet facilities. Another option is the limited but reasonably priced ($28.50 single, $33.50 double) accommodations available on the base. Make reservations by calling the Billeting Office at 831-386-2511. For information and a hunter packet, contact the address above.

Call 831-386-3310 for a recorded message anytime. If you want to talk to a real person (which is often difficult), call 831-386-2677 between 3 and 7 P.M. on Friday or Saturday, and between 5 A.M. and 6 P.M. on Sundays.

Fee-Access Private Hunting Areas

As previously mentioned, most wild hogs in California are killed on private lands. Your chances are simply better there. In the case of fee-access hunts, success ranges from a few percent to more than 50 percent, depending on where you hunt, how much time you put in, your skill level, etc. However, for these better odds, you will pay a price. Fee-access private areas are cheaper than guided hunts, but a fee is required. You may be able to locate a private ranch that charges a trespass fee—for the year or for a specified number of days. These trespass-fee places are generally discovered by word of mouth, and some advertise or are mentioned in sportsmen's newspapers including *Western Outdoor News*, *Fishing and Hunting News*, and the *California Hog Hunter* newsletter (see Appendix A for more details). Additionally, there are organizations that control access on a number of hog properties in California and offer hunting on a seasonal membership basis.

Wilderness Unlimited is one of several organizations that offer hunting on a seasonal membership basis and control access to properties in California that support wild hogs. They maintain from 100,000 to 150,000 acres that support wild pigs.

Not only are lots of wild pigs killed on private land, but hunter success is consistently high—often running 90 percent or better. Even hunters with their sights set on a trophy boar with good tusks can count on a 40-percent success rate on the better ranches. Scott Currier poses with a trophy boar taken on private property.

Golden Ram Sportsmen's Club
321 Endless Ct., El Dorado Hills, CA 95762
916-941-7880
Web site: www.goldenramhunting.com

This club has been around for thirty years and currently leases about 100,000 acres for hunting everything from upland birds to deer. Two of the ranches, totaling about 30,000 acres, support good hog populations. One is in Sonoma County near Healsburg, north of Sonoma Lake, and the other is in San Luis Obispo County near Paso Robles. Both offer good populations of meat hogs and a reasonable number of trophy animals. Hunter success is at least 50 percent, provided you put your time in.

Though the pig season is year-round, Golden Ram restricts hog hunting to October through January and April through June. By February the roads generally get muddy and access becomes difficult; July through September is the coastal deer season. Each property has a quota, and hunters sign up by calling the Golden Ram office. About the only time access to these ranches might be a problem is opening weekend of deer season. Otherwise, according to Golden Ram owner Nick Tacito, entry is virtually guaranteed. To join the Golden Ram Sportsmen's Club, there is a onetime membership fee that starts at $1,000, along with annual dues ranging from $1,000 (individual) to $2,600 (corporate).

White Deer Ranch
13753 Highway 140, Livingston, CA 95334
209-394-7423

The White Deer Ranch is a 6,000-acre property located twenty-eight miles east of Fresno in the Sierra foothills near Dunlap. The habitat is rolling to steep, mostly oak woodland, annual grassland, and manzanita brush. The ranch, managed by Red Delaney, switched in 2001 from guided hunts to fee-access hunts. An annual membership fee allows all-year access and hunting. White Deer holds fair to good populations of wild pigs along with deer, wild turkeys, upland birds, and varmints. Some boars that top 300 pounds roam the place.

The cost of an annual membership is $5,000 and entitles the member and one guest to unlimited hunting privileges. State bag limits are in effect for all species, and Delaney does not restrict the number of hogs each member can take. The membership fee allows camping on the ranch as well as the use of a historic ranch house (bring your own food and bedding). There are motels and restaurants in Squaw Valley eight miles west.

Wilderness Unlimited
20974 Corsair Blvd., Hayward, CA 94545
510-785-HUNT (4868)
Web site: www.wildernessunlimited.com

This sportsmen's organization is in the business of leasing and managing property specifically for hunting, fishing, and camping, with properties in California and Oregon. In California, it manages more than 350,000 acres on eighty-five properties that provide trout and warm-water fishing and hunting for everything from doves to deer to wild hogs. Members and their guests access the properties and hunt on their own.

Each property has a maximum number of hunters that can be there at one time. Members call the Wilderness Unlimited office to make reservations. The signups are generally first-call, first-served until the property quota is reached. In rare cases, like the opening day of deer season, a drawing among interested members may be held to select who gets on. Access is generally not a problem for pig hunters because the state season is year-round. Wilderness Unlimited does, however, have a self-imposed closed pig season from 1 June to mid-July.

Currently, the outfit has twenty-four ranches totaling 115,000 acres that support wild pigs. Four of them are open to bow hunters only. The number of properties and total acres available are subject to change each year, but traditionally the pig-hunting places range from 100,000 to 150,000 acres. Hunter success varies widely, but according to Wilderness Unlimited president Rick Copeland, hunters who work hard have at least a 50 percent chance of success. Each property is rated as good, fair, or poor based or recent wildlife sightings and hunting success.

Wilderness Unlimited has a onetime enrollment fee that ranges from $500 to $1,000 (depending on type of membership) along with an annual fee of $500 and up. Membership includes access to all properties for fishing, hunting, camping, and just getting away. Most ranches have primitive campsites while others have developed campsites with portable bathrooms and water.

Guided and Semi-Guided Hunts on Private Land

During the 1999–2000 license year, 90.9 percent of the wild hogs killed in California were harvested on private land. Hunter success, too, is consistently high on private lands, often running 90 percent or better on a two-day guided hunt. Even hunters with their sights set on a trophy boar with good tusks can count on 40 percent success on the better ranches. This level of success, of course, will require you to open up your wallet and lay down some cash. Typically, hunts are two days, although some guides offer shorter or longer ones. Included in the price is access to private land, hunting services including guide fees, and in some cases meals and accommodations. For these services, guides/outfitters charge $150 to $500 a day. Some guides charge for guiding only and leave the motel and meals up to you. Trophy and kill fees are often levied in addition to the base price of

About 90 percent of the wild hogs killed in California are harvested on private land. These hunts include access to private land, hunting services including guide fees, and, in some cases, meals and accommodations. Hunter Mike Bruno poses with guide Jim Settle with a nice boar taken on Dye Creek Preserve.

the hunt and range from $100 and up for meat hogs to $150 and up for trophy boars with tusks longer than two inches. Private-land hunts on the better ranches are often booked well in advance. Even two-day guided hunts with all the amenities on the most expensive ranches are often booked months in advance, particularly from mid-January to mid-July, when other hunting seasons are closed.

Though I have made an effort to contact the majority of guides and outfitters who offer wild-pig hunting in California, the list below is not all-inclusive. Also, the information in this section is designed to be accurate as of April 2002. I have personally hunted with some of the outfitters listed here, but this section should not be considered an endorsement of every guide operation or ranch listed. For a complete list of guides, contact the California Department of Fish and Game, License and Revenue Branch, 3311 S St., Sacramento, CA 95816; 916-227-2177; Web site: www.dfg.ca.gov/licensing.

Sacramento Valley

Antelope Valley Hunt Club
4165 LaGrande Rd., Williams, CA 95987
530-473-2790; fax 530-473-2076

Owned and operated by John Alvernaz, this club has two properties in Colusa County, a 6,000-acre ranch about six miles west of Sites, and 2,000 acres ten miles northwest of Williams. The larger property is an operating cattle ranch, and the habitat is oak woodland, annual grassland, and chamise brushlands. The smaller property is on the edge of the valley floor and is a combination of oak savanna, some brush, and agricultural land devoted to rice, rowcrops, and almond orchards.

Alvernaz has been offering hog hunts on both properties for about six years. The hunting is spot-and-stalk, and over the years hunter success has averaged 90 percent. Hunts are available all year, and the bag is a nice mix of meat animals and trophy boars. During the hot summer months the hogs are concentrated near water, particularly on the smaller property, where the hunting generally requires very little walking. The hogs are more scattered during the winter and early spring, when the grass is green, and that is Alvernaz's favorite time to hunt them. The weather is generally mild, lots of hogs are seen, and the extra effort required makes the kill even more rewarding. Alvernaz charges $150 a day for guided hunts, with an additional kill fee of $250 for meat hogs and $450 for trophy boars with tusks longer than two inches.

Burrows Ranch
12250 Colyear Springs Rd., Red Bluff, CA 96080
530-529-1535
e-mail: burrows@cwnet.com

Bill Burrows has been offering guided pig hunts on his 3,500-acre Tehama County ranch for the past fifteen years. The ranch, located twenty-five miles southwest of Red Bluff, is a mixture of oak woodland, annual grassland, and brush. Burrows offers spot-and-stalk hunting all yearlong, and his clients average 95-plus percent success. In 2001, fifty wild hogs that averaged 176 pounds were harvested. Burrows points out that most of the pigs killed are 140- to 170-pound meat animals, though a few larger boars are present. Burrows Ranch offers full-service hunts that include lodging, meals, and all hunting services. Prices are $450 per hunter in groups of three, $475 in groups of two, and $600 for a single hunter. There is no additional trophy fee. Deer, wild turkey, dove, quail, and varmint hunting are available as well.

California Wild Sports
1807 6th St., Lincoln, CA 95648
916-434-9555

Pat Flaherty recently acquired the hunting rights on a 7,500-acre ranch in Colusa County fifteen miles west of Williams. He has been guiding for years, but 2002 is his first year on the new property. The habitat is chamise brush, annual grassland, and scattered oaks. Flaherty offers spot-and-stalk hunting from October to the end of April, and his clients average 95-plus percent success. There is a good mix of meat hogs and trophy boars, including some that top 300 pounds. Two-day hunts are a flat rate of $450 for any pig. Hunters stay in Williams, where there are motels and restaurants. Flaherty also guides for deer and exotic sheep and goats.

Dye Creek Preserve
Multiple Use Managers
P.O. Box 669, Los Molinos, CA 96055
800-557-7087
Web site: www.mumwildlife.com

Some of the best hog hunting in California is on the Dye Creek Preserve, a 37,000-acre ranch near Red Bluff in Tehama County. The ranch is operated by TNC, and the hunting is managed by Multiple Use Managers. For many years the property was a private cattle ranch, but in 1987 its oversight shifted to TNC. Today, cattle grazing, hunting, environmental education, and various wildlife research projects are all part of the operation. Wayne Long obtained the original hunting lease back in the mid-1960s, and his company operated all aspects of the hunting program between 1965 and 1973 and again from 1986 to the present. Long's son, Gordy, is currently the on-site manager.

Wild-pig hunting is permitted on Dye Creek between 1 December and 30 May. There are plenty of meat hogs along with a respectable number of trophy boars; it's common to see fifty pigs during the course of a two-day hunt. The hunting is strictly spot-and-stalk, and the habitat is a mixture of blue-oak/foothill pine woodlands, open grasslands, and dense brush. During the winter months the pigs are found in the middle and upper elevations, where they feed heavily on acorns, green grasses, and tubers. In the spring, as the weather warms, the acorns disappear, and grasses dry up, the hogs move down to the riparian areas, where there is better water and feed. Hunter success on Dye Creek averages 95 percent. A two-day hunt is $700 per hunter, entitling you to one hog, ranch-house accommodations, meals, and hunting services. There is a $200 trophy fee for boars with tusks two inches and longer. Dye Creek also offers deer, waterfowl, and upland bird hunting in season.

Lassen Gun and Guides
P.O. Box 1483, Susanville, CA 96130
530-257-7454

Mark A. Paul owns and operates Lassen Gun and Guides. He has been hunting for thirty years and guiding full-time for the past fifteen years. He hunts hogs on two ranches totaling about 10,000 acres. One of the properties, fifteen miles west of Red Bluff in Tehama County, is dominated by brushlands with scattered oaks and annual grasslands. The other ranch is near the Mendocino/Trinity County line, twenty-five miles northwest of Covelo, where the habitat is oak woodland, chamise brushlands, grasslands, and some conifer forest. He does a lot of spot-and-stalk hunting but also uses dogs to bay pigs. Meat hogs average 130 to 150 pounds while most trophy boars run 200 to 250 pounds. The largest taken by one of Paul's clients tipped the scales at 350 pounds. Over the years, 95-plus percent of his clients have taken a pig.

Paul offers two-day hunts for meat hogs (no meals or accommodations) for $675, meat-hog hunts that include two nights lodging and meals for $870, and trophy boar hunts with room and board for $995. This outfit is well known for its pronghorn antelope (Zones 4 and 5), deer (X6A, X5B, M-8, A-11), and bear hunts.

Richard Duncan
3083 Brim Rd., Williams, CA 95987
530-473-5047

Though Rich Duncan has been hunting hogs for nearly twenty-five years, only in the past four has he offered guided hunts on his 1,200-acre ranch twenty-five miles west of Williams on the Colusa/Lake County line. The habitat is chamise brush and annual grassland with scattered oaks. Hunting, available year-round, is a combination of spot-and-stalk and still hunting. In the winter, the hogs bed down in traditional locations, and still hunting can be effective. During the warmer months, spot-and-stalk is the preferred method, and hogs can often be patterned as they move between feeding and watering areas. Hunter success averages 50 to 60 percent. Duncan offers some of the least-expensive guided pig hunting in California: Half-day hunts are $100, full-day hunts $150. There is no kill fee for meat hogs, but it's $200 (plus $100 per inch over two inches) for trophy boars.

Rocky Ridge Hunting Club
P.O. Box 8552, Red Bluff, CA 96080
530-200-1925 or 1926

Tom and Crystal Burrill have operated Rocky Ridge Hunting Club on their 30,000-acre ranch for the past ten years. An operating cattle ranch about thirty miles due west of Red Bluff in Tehama County, it's a mixture of oak woodland, annual grassland, and manzanita brush. Crystal does most of the guiding and is an avid hunter herself. Tom guides when the client load requires it. They can take care of up to ten hunters a day. The hunting is spot-and-stalk, and success averages 95 percent. The hogs are mostly meat pigs, with a few trophy boars present. In a typical day, you should see three or four groups of hogs that can number as many as fifty. The hunting areas are generally reached on ATVs, but horses and four-wheel-drive vehicles are available as well. Two-day packages go for a flat rate of $500 per person, which includes meals and accommodations in a ranch house on the property.

North Coast

Arrow Five Outfitters
Star Rt. 1, Box 64A, Zenia, CA 95595
707-923-9633
e-mail: arrow5@cwnet.com

Arrow Five is owned and operated by Jim and Tina Marie Schaafsma, who have offered guided hog hunting in northern California for years on a 12,000-acre ranch in Trinity County about thirty miles east of Garberville. The habitat is a mixture of riparian areas and oak woodland along with brush and evergreen forest at the higher elevations. About 75 percent of the hogs are killed using dogs, the remainder by spot-and-stalkers. Dogs often make the difference between success and failure here.

Hog hunting is available from 10 February to 30 May, and the cost of a 2½-day hunt is $750 for one person, $700 per hunter

All pigs have a naked, fleshy snout used to root out bulbs, roots, nuts, and insects. An area that has been rooted or dug up is a positive sign that hogs are using the area. This hog has just finished rooting and still has dirt on its nose

in parties of two, and $650 per hunter for a group of three to five. The package includes accommodations, meals, and hunting services. Women-only hunts are also an option. Hunter success is about 80 percent; taking a meat hog is seldom a problem. The ranch also produces trophy black-tailed deer, and in December and January the owners run a Coues deer hunt in Sonora, Mexico.

Circle F Ranch
23337 Fish Rock Rd., Yorkville, CA 95494
707-895-3895

This 4,000-acre ranch about fifteen miles southwest of Booneville in Mendocino County is operated by Kevin FioRito, who has been guiding on the north coast since the early 1980s. The habitat is fairly open oak savanna with steep canyons, scattered redwood groves, and brushlands. The hunts are strictly spot-and-stalk, and only boars can be taken. Those harvested in recent years have been a good mix of meat pigs and trophies, including several in the 250-plus-pound class. FioRito offers pig hunts all year, but says hunting is most productive and enjoyable in the fall, when the hogs are feeding on acorns, and during the winter and early spring, when they move into the open areas to root. Over the years, hunter success has been 80 to 85 percent, with most clients getting a shot. Circle F offers two-day hunts for $450, including access to the ranch and guide service, and there is no additional fee when a kill is made. Clients can camp on the ranch for free, and there is a bunkhouse available for $50 a night for two people or $75 for three or four. Motels and restaurants are available in Ukiah. In addition to pigs, Circle F offers wild turkeys, A-Zone deer, varmints, and upland birds.

Craig's Guide Service and Outfitters
P.O. Box 188, Kelseyville, CA 95451
707-279-0422

Craig Van Housen has been guiding on the north coast since the late 1970s and offers hog hunting on two ranches in Mendocino County, one south and one west of Ukiah. Combined, they cover about 9,000 acres. The habitat is typical north-coast oak woodland, with conifers at the higher elevations along with some brush and annual grasslands. The terrain varies from rolling hills to steep slopes. Van Housen offers two types of hunts. The first is a self-guided option in which he provides access to the ranches, a map, and a radio. He goes over the lay of the land with you and points out recent pig sightings. During the day, Van Housen checks on the hunters, and when a hog is killed, he goes in and helps pack it out. The price of the unguided hunts is $175 a day per hunter with a two-hunter minimum. Success on these hunts averages about 50 percent, and a lot of it depends on your physical condition and hunting savvy. Van Housen also offers guided hunting with stock dogs. These run $200 a day per hunter, with an additional $200 when a pig is taken. Hunter success on the dog hunts is 90 to 95 percent. Meat hogs average right around 125 pounds and the trophy boars 200, both weights typical for this region. Hunts run from 1 October to 30 May. Most hunters stay in Ukiah.

Hillside Hog Haven
Skaggs Spring Rd., Annapolis, CA 95412
707-847-3727

Robert Larson has been guiding on the same ranch in Sonoma County for the past twelve years. The ranch, about twelve miles east of Stewarts Point and thirty miles west of Healdsburg in prime pig country, covers 4,000 acres of oak woodland, madrone, and chamise brushlands along with stands of redwood and Douglas fir on the ridges. Larson offers archery hunting only and is an avid bow hunter himself. He uses spot-and-stalk and still hunting, and his place has a good mix of trophy boars and meat hogs. The boars seem to be more approachable—a critical requirement for bow hunters—in the fall around Thanksgiving and again in the spring, coinciding with the two main rutting periods on the north coast. Larson's clients have enjoyed about 50 percent hunter success, which is excellent for bow hunters. And while he can't guarantee anything, he says that 99 percent of his hunters get within a few yards of a pig. He charges $350 for day hunts ($400 if it's an afternoon followed by a morning) and $450 for a day hunt that includes use of a cabin. You'll have to bring your own food, but there are hot showers and all the other comforts of home. He allows only one or two hunters per day on the ranch.

Miller Ranch Outfitters
P.O. Box 31, Laytonville, CA 95454
707-984-6092

Richard Eriksen guides on a 1,000-acre ranch about six miles east of Laytonville in Mendocino County. Like much of the north coast, the habitat is a mix of timbered ridges, oak woodlands, annual grasslands, and chamise brush. Eriksen offers only archery hunting, year-round. The hunts are semiguided; he shows you the lay of the land and then points you in the right direction. When you get a hog down, he will help you get it out. Hunter success runs about 60 percent, which is at the top of the scale for semiguided archery hunts. Eriksen charges $350 for a two-day hunt, including use of a rustic cabin (bring your own food and sleeping bags), or you can go into Laytonville, where there are motels and restaurants. Eriksen also guides for deer and wild turkeys.

Mountain Bound
5115 Todd Rd., Sebastapol, CA 95472
707-829-1117

Mike Patt runs Mountain Bound, an archery-only operation in Sonoma County, on one of the smallest hog-hunting ranches in the state, a 500-acre property about five miles south of Lake Sonoma. The terrain is rolling, and the habitat is oak woodland, annual grassland, and chamise brush. The hunting is spot-and-stalk and still hunting. Patt hunts all year but likes the fall months, when the hogs are concentrated and feeding on acorns, and the spring, when they venture out to feed on green grass. His clients succeed 50 to 60 percent of the time. Patt charges a flat rate of $200 a day for a guided archery hunt. Hunters stay in Healdsburg. Mountain Bound also offers spring wild turkey hunts.

Redwood Empire Outdoor Adventures
P.O. Box 757, Miranda, CA 95553
707-943-3003
e-mail: kdbowman@asis.com

Ken Bowman has owned and operated this outfit since 1989. He guides on two ranches that total 7,000 acres. The majority of the hogs are taken on the 5,800-acre Island Mountain Trinity Ranch near the Mendocino/Trinity County line, about twenty miles east of Harris and forty miles southeast of Garberville. The terrain varies from rolling hills to steep slopes and is a mix of oak woodland, open meadows, brush, and conifer stands. Spot-and-stalk hunts are offered from August to December and March to the end of May. His hunters enjoy success in the 80 to 90 percent range.

Two-day hunts are $500 per hunter and include accommodations, meals, and all hunting services. Redwood Empire is in the process of building a hunting lodge on the Island Mountain property, and it should be ready for clients sometime in 2002. Bowman does not charge a trophy fee, but he was straightforward in pointing out to me that while trophy boars are present, they don't make up a large percentage of the hogs taken. Bowman also guides for deer, turkeys, and quail.

Solitude Guide Service
3557 Piner Rd., Santa Rosa, CA 95401
707-545-7049

Scott Galloway operates Solitude and has been guiding on the north coast since the early 1980s. He hunts on a 20,000-acre ranch in Sonoma County west of Cloverdale. Much of the ranch is oak woodland, with some brush in the draws and grasslands on the benches. He offers three types of hunting: guided hunts with dogs, guided spot-and-stalk, and unguided spot-and-stalk. On the unguided hunts, Galloway shows you where he has seen hogs, then turns you loose. When you kill a pig, he'll help you get it out. On the unguided hunts, about a third of the clients take home a pig. Hunter success on the guided hunts generally hits 90 percent. The hunts are offered November through May. Most meat hogs fall in the 125- to 150-pound class while trophy boars run 200 to 250 pounds. One-day guided hunts (dogs or spot-and-stalk) are $200 per day, plus $200 when a kill is made. The unguided hunts are $175 per day, and there is no kill fee. In addition to pigs, Solitude Guide Service offers dog hunts for bears and bobcats and spring turkey hunting.

West Coast Adventures
1014 Hopper Ave., Santa Rosa, CA 95403
707-579-3078

West Coast Adventures is owned and operated by Scott Young, who guides on three ranches, two in Lake County and one in Sonoma

County. He has been at it for fifteen years, and hog hunting is second nature with him. The Sonoma property, about 2,000 acres in the Healdsburg area, is rolling hills covered with oak woodland, grassland, and brush. Here the hunting is exclusively spot-and-stalk. The two Lake County ranches combined cover about 18,000 acres in the Lower Lake area and are a bit more brushy and there is more relief to the terrain. There, Young uses stock dogs to bay the pigs. Overall, about 75 percent of the pigs are taken with the help of dogs, and the rest are spot-and-stalk. Day hunts cost $250, plus $200 when a pig is taken. Meat hogs in the 100- to 130-pound range are available, as are trophy boars that regularly top 200 pounds. The Sonoma ranch hunters stay in Healdsburg; those hunting in Lake County stay at Lower Lake or at the Konocti Resort. Young is an avid archer, and many of his clients take pigs with archery equipment. Over the years, hunter success has averaged 75 percent overall, higher for hunts using dogs. Young runs hog hunts from December through April.

Wild Pig Hunting/Ken Whittaker
P.O. Box 260, Yorkville, CA 95494
707-894-3280
e-mail: adwhit@juno.com

As the company name indicates, guide Ken Whittaker concentrates on one thing—wild pigs. He's been at it for nearly thirty years, having started his guide business in the early 1970s. He has acquired the hog-hunting rights on a 20,000-acre ranch about five miles due west of Cloverdale. Half of the ranch is in Sonoma County and the other half in Mendocino. The habitat is dominated by chamise brushlands mixed with oak woodlands and, in some areas, redwood trees. The property is adjacent to Lake Sonoma, and a portion of the original ranch was flooded when the COE built the lake back in the 1960s. The ranch borders the Sonoma Wildlife Area, where a public hunting program mentioned earlier is operated by the CDF&G. Many of the pigs killed on the public area spend much of their time on Whittaker's lease. Whittaker offers two distinctly different types of hunting. The first is a semiguided spot-and-stalk hunt, showing hunters the lay of the land and where the pigs have been hanging out. Once he feels comfortable you won't get lost, he drops you off and you're on your own. Over the years, on-your-own clients have enjoyed 25 to 50 percent success. The fee for the semiguided hunt is $175 a day or $300 for two days. The other option is a guided hunt with dogs; fees are $200 a day per hunter, with an additional $200 fee if a pig is killed. Success using dogs is about 80 percent.

Whittaker offers hunts from 1 October to 30 May. The hunting is particularly good and the hogs are in prime condition in the fall and early winter, after they have spent several weeks fattening on acorns. Hunters stay in motels in Healdsburg or Cloverdale, camp on the ranch, or stay at the Liberty Glenn Public Campground, just down the road and adjacent to Lake Sonoma.

Central Coast

Anderson Taxidermy and Guide Service
13600 Old Morro Rd., Atascadero, CA 93442
805-466-3240
email: andersontaxidermy@thegrid.net

Don Anderson has been guiding for eighteen years and hunts on three ranches. Two are in San Luis Obispo County and total 4,500 acres; the third is a 10,000-acre ranch in Ventura County. The terrain on the San Luis ranches is rolling hills with a mixture of oak savanna, annual grassland, and chaparral brush plus some pasture ground and barley fields. One ranch is located two miles northeast of Parkfield, and the other is near Santa Margarita Lake. Spot-and-stalk hunting is offered all year, and hunter success averages 80-plus percent, with a nice mix of meat and trophy animals. Anderson charges $150 a day plus a $400 kill fee for any hog. Hunters generally stay in Parkfield at the Parkfield Inn or drive fifteen miles from the Santa Margarita ranch to Atascadero, where there are motels and restaurants.

The Ventura County ranch is eight miles southeast of the city of Ventura, and the habitat is oak woodland, annual grassland, brush, and citrus and avocado orchards. Anderson operates this property as a bowhunting club. A one-year membership is $1,300, and up to five hogs can be harvested. Anderson also offers deer, wild turkey, and exotic sheep hunting on the central coast and guides for brown bears in Alaska and exotics in Texas.

Boar Busters Guide Service
P.O. Box 41, San Lucas, CA 93954
831-382-4837

Boar Busters operates on two ranches totaling 21,000 acres east of Highway 101 between San Lucas and San Ardo in Monterey County. Teddy McCormack owns the outfit and has been in the business for five years. The ranches, 18,000 and 3,000 acres, are a mixture of oak savanna, annual grassland, and chamise brush typical of the central coast. About 900 acres are planted to barley, which is the primary food for wild hogs between April and October. The ranches also support cattle, which are provided supplemental feed (barley and carrots) from June to November. Hogs are attracted to that feed and are easy to pattern. The hunting is about 70 percent spot-and-stalk and 30 percent with dogs. Hunter success runs 95-plus percent. McCormack charges a flat rate of $400 for a two-day hunt and does not charge a trophy fee. The ratio of meat pigs to trophy boars is about ten to one, with some boars in the 250-plus-pound class harvested each year. A cabin on one of the ranches will accommodate four to five hunters and rents for $250 a weekend. You'll have to bring your own food and bedding. There are plenty of motels and restaurants in King City, about fifteen miles away. Hunts are offered all year, with the most consistent action from April through November. McCormack also offers varmint hunts.

Boaring Experiences
P.O. Box 398, Atascadero, CA 93423
805-461-0294 [voice/fax]
Web site: www.boaring.com

Kyler Hamann has owned and operated Boaring Experiences since 1988 and hunts hogs all year on nine ranches totaling about 32,000 acres in Monterey and San Luis Obispo counties. The habitat is chaparral brush, oak woodlands, and cultivated areas where barley is the primary crop, a combination that supports good wild-hog populations. The hunting is spot-and-stalk; no dogs are permitted. In the spring and summer, most hunters wait and watch for hogs as they leave the barley fields in the morning or head for them in the late afternoon. In the fall and early winter, the action shifts to the oak woodlands, where the hogs feed on acorns. Boaring Experiences offers one-day guided hunts for $175, plus a $250 kill fee. A two-day/two-night package is available for $750 and includes hunting services, one hog, and meals and accommodations at a local inn. If you take a hog (meat or trophy) on a two-day package, there is no additional fee. Over the years, Hamann's clients have enjoyed a 60 to 100 percent success rate. The best hunting is in late spring and summer. During the winter months, the hogs are more spread out and the hunting more difficult. Both meat hogs and trophy boars—some weighing more than 300 pounds—are taken each year. Varmint, upland birds, and deer are offered in season.

Busby's Hog Service
165 Old Stage Rd., Salinas, CA 93908
831-443-5864

Wayne Busby, who has been in the business for ten years, operates on five ranches totaling about 18,000 acres in Monterey and San Benito counties between Lockwood and San Jose off Highway 101. In typical central-coast habitat, Busby hunts exclusively with dogs, and over the years hunter success has been better than 90 percent. The hunts are offered all year, and though the dogs find pigs every month of the year, the cooler months from October to May are easier on the dogs—and the hunters. Busby charges a flat rate of $400 a day, and you're on your own for meals and lodging. Clients stay in King City, Salinas, or San Jose.

Call Mountain Guide Service
1600 Old Airline Hwy., Paicines, CA 95043
831-389-4535 or 831-663-4346

Jack Clark and Steve Sweet have been partners since the early 1970s and have been guiding hog hunters ever since. Currently, they hunt on a 13,000-acre cattle ranch southeast of Hollister on the edge of the Diablo Range in San Benito County. The countryside is rolling to steep and is a combination of annual grasslands, oak woodland, and brush. In the morning, spot-and-stalk is the preferred method; in the afternoon, dogs are often pressed into service to find pigs in the heavy cover and bay them—then it's up to you to catch up to them before the pig decides to cut and run.

Beyond the requirement that a centerfire rifle or pistol cartridge be used when hunting wild pigs, the selection of the weapon, caliber, and bullet are yours. Jim Settle poses with a trophy boar taken with a .270 bolt-action rifle on the Dye Creek Preserve.

Clark recommends open-sight rifles for shooting pigs when dogs are involved. Pistols can be used, but they must be in the hands of a seasoned handgun shooter, he cautioned, or it's too dangerous! Clark and Sweet hunt from early October to late April, avoiding the hot summer months. Over the years, hunter success has been at least 95 percent, with a nice mix of meat hogs and trophy boars. Two-day hunts that include room and board are $300 per hunter, and one-day hunts that include lunches are $200; add $200 when you shoot a pig.

Camp 5 Outfitters
1230 Arbor Dr., Paso Robles, CA 93446
831-386-0727
e-mail: droth@tcsn.net

This organization has been guiding hog hunters in the central-coast region since 1985. Owned and operated by Doug Roth, Camp 5 can field five guides and hunts on six different ranches totaling about 50,000 acres. The properties lie between Paso Robles and King City, and the habitat is a mixture of oak woodland, chaparral, annual grasslands, and cultivated barley.

The hunting is spot-and-stalk, and the hogs use the barley fields from planting time in early spring until harvest in late summer. Most trophy hogs weigh 200 to 300 pounds, and meat hogs average 150. Both are present in good numbers, and over the years hunter success has been 90 percent or better. Each year, Camp 5 takes about 300 pigs, making it one of the larger operators on the central coast.

Two-day hunts are $700, and there is no trophy fee when a hog is killed. If you take a pig on the first day, ground squirrel and coyote hunting are available for no additional charge. The price includes hunting services but not meals or lodging. There are accommodations ($50 a night per person) with kitchen facilities on three of the ranches. If you want meals catered and delivered, meals and lodging are an additional $150 a day per person. Otherwise, there are plenty of places to stay and eat within a reasonable driving distance. Camp 5 also offers deer, turkey, and varmint hunting in season and operates a pheasant preserve.

Carnaza Hunting Adventures
7373 Carnaza Rd., Santa Margarita, CA 93453
805-475-2341

Alex and Lisa Kuhnle have been operating Carnaza Hunting Adventures for fifteen years. They hunt on a 10,000-acre home ranch and four other properties for a total of 30,000 acres, primarily in San Luis Obispo County along Highway 58 between Santa Margarita and Bakersfield. The habitat is varied and includes oak woodlands, annual grasslands, juniper brushlands, and agricultural lands planted to wheat and barley. The hunting is entirely spot-and-stalk, and though guided hunting is available all year, some of the best action coincides with the maturing of the grain crops. The wheat and barley start to form seed heads in late May, and enough is left on the ground after the harvest to attract hogs to the fields until late September or early October. The hunting is good the rest of the year, too, but the hogs are not as concentrated. Hunting success is high—only a couple of hunters went home without a hog in the past decade. Two-day hunts are a flat rate of $450 for meat hogs and $500 for trophy boars, including all hunting services, lunch, cold drinks in the field, and overnight accommodations in a trailer on the home ranch. Some hunters prefer to stay in a motel and drive forty-five miles west to Paso Robles or San Luis Obispo.

Cross Country Outfitters
P.O. Box 3904, Paso Robles, CA 93447
805-467-3947
Web site: www.tcsn.net/crosscountry

Owners August and Tom Harden, who have been in the hog-hunting business for fifteen years, have four ranches that cover about 35,000 acres. With an annual harvest of up to 150 pigs, they are serious players in the central-coast hog-hunting scene. The properties are within thirty miles of Paso Robles and are mostly oak woodland and annual grasslands, along with some chamise brush and agricultural areas devoted primarily to barley and wheat. The Hardens hunt only hogs, and it's mostly spot-and-stalk, although they do a fair amount of still hunting, particularly during the summer months. While pig hunting is available and productive every month of the year, hogs are the most concentrated from May through September. This time period coincides with the ripening and harvest of the grain fields and provides the best opportunity to look at multiple animals before taking a shot. This also is when most of the trophy boars are killed. Cross Country offers two-day pig hunts for a flat rate of $500, and according to August Harden, if you haven't killed your hog by the second day, he will refund half the money. He also told me that it's a rare day when he sends a hunter home empty-handed—the success rate is 95-plus percent.

Devil's Canyon Guide Service
10945 Old Hernandez Rd., Paicines, CA 95043
831-385-6155
e-mail: Boarslayers_R_us@yahoo.com

Owned and operated by Mike Baumgartner, this outfit holds hog hunts on a 7,000-acre ranch about thirty miles east of King City in San Benito County. He has been guiding on this ranch for the past five years. Oak savanna and brush dominate the landscape, and about six miles of the San Benito River flow through the property. Add 1,500 acres of barley, wheat, corn, and alfalfa, and you have wild-hog heaven. The hunts are spot-and-stalk, and hunter success runs 95-plus percent. If a trophy boar is your quarry, a high percentage of the animals on the ranch will qualify. Devil's Canyon offers hunts all year, with the most productive months being May through September. Two-day guided hunts that include cabin accommodations but no food are $550 in groups of two to five hunters or $700 for a single hunter. There is no additional kill fee. Baumgartner also offers deer, turkey, and upland bird hunts.

Easterbrook Ranch/Boar's Breath Guide Service
69621 Vineyard Canyon Rd., San Miguel, CA 93451
805-463-2476
e-mail: easterbrook@bigplanet.com

Located about two miles north of Parkfield, the Easterbrook Ranch at 800 acres is the smallest property in the central-coast lineup. It is run by Andy and Sheryl Easterbrook; the guiding is done by Andy Easterbrook or Jeff Wolcott (Jeff operates under the Boar's Breath Guide Service name). Guided hog hunts have been offered here for ten years. The habitat is oak woodland mixed with annual grassland and brush, and it's loaded with hogs. There are barley fields nearby, and the ranch has good water. The hunting is spot-and-stalk, and most of the hunters get a chance for a shot. Repeat business runs about 80 percent. The bag is a nice mix of meat hogs and trophy boars. Two-day hunts (weekends only, all year) that include cabin accommodations (bring your sleeping bag, food, and water) are $500. They also offer A-Zone deer hunts and combo deer/pig hunts.

Eldon Bergman Guide Service
P.O. Box 1175, Templeton, CA 93465
805-238-5504

Eldon Bergman has been guiding pig hunters for so long (forty years) that many consider him the Godfather of California hog hunting. Currently, he offers hunts on two ranches totaling 20,500 acres east of Paso Robles. As you might guess, he knows the ranches intimately and sees pigs virtually every day in the field. The habitat is typical central-coast oak savanna and brush, along with dryland barley and oats. At one time Bergman used dogs, but in recent years he has switched to strictly spot-and-stalk. He charges $350 a day, including one meat hog, and a boar with two-inch or longer tusks will cost you an additional $200. He generally guides three days per week, and most of his hunters are successful in one day. The hunting is most consistent spring through fall. Hunter success averages about 80 percent.

Golden Tusk Guide Service
224 Panorama Dr., Paso Robles, CA 93446
805-434-0757 or 805-238-2498

Golden Tusk is owned and operated by Steve Wells, a guide on the central coast for ten years and formerly an apprentice under Eldon Bergman. Steve hunts all year on two ranches totaling about 4,000 acres, one in Monterey County ten miles east of San Miguel and the other in San Luis Obispo County ten miles east of Paso

Robles off Highway 46. The habitat is oak savanna, annual grassland, chamise brush, and dryland barley, providing a good mix of meat pigs and trophy boars. The Monterey County ranch has flowing water all year and barley fields, making it a good producer of pigs. The San Luis Obispo property is good all year as well, with winter months the most productive. The two ranches are close enough that you can hunt both in the same day if necessary. The hunting is spot-and-stalk, and virtually every hunter gets a shot. Wells charges $200 for a 2½-day hunt, plus a $300 kill fee for meat hogs and $350 and up for big boars, depending on size. Wells offers rain checks—if you are unsuccessful the first time out, you can come back and pay only the kill fee when successful. The hunts include some meals but no accommodations. Hunters generally stay in Paso Robles, ten miles west of the San Luis Obispo ranch and thirty miles southwest of the Monterey County ranch. Wells also guides for deer, turkeys, and upland birds.

Helicopter Fly-in Hunting Service
327 West Rossi St., Salinas, CA 93907
831-422-1521
Web site: www.helicopterflyinhunting.com

Without a doubt, Vic Massolo operates a unique pig-hunting operation. He offers semiguided hunts on public land not accessible to the general public. In 1998 Massolo came up with the helicopter fly-in idea. He knew there were good populations of wild pigs and deer on public land, but many of the parcels were "landlocked"— surrounded by private land. And as we all know, the chances of getting permission to cross private land to access public land are slim to none! The only other way to reach these parcels (up to 20,000 acres) was by air, and without an airstrip, the only way in was by helicopter. So Massolo put together Helicopter Fly-in Hunting Service and offers hunts on hundreds of thousands of acres of BLM land in Monterey, San Benito, and Fresno counties. Thanks to the difficult access, you might be working land that has seen only a handful of hunters in the past decade. The habitat ranges from oak woodland and oak savanna to dense chaparral brushlands and annual grasslands.

The hunts last a minimum of two and a maximum of four days—you decide how long you want to be out. The package includes one night's accommodation in Massolo's ranch house in Salinas and dinner the night before the hunt. The chopper takes off the next day with the hunters, food, water, and tents and flies anywhere from minutes to more than an hour from Salinas to one of these landlocked parcels. He takes a minimum of two and a maximum of four hunters. Massolo doesn't technically guide, but he knows the parcels and gives you a radio and sends you where he knows the hogs live. He flies in with you to set up camp, then stays there to make sure all goes well. He even helps pack out the animals you shoot. When it's all done, the camp is gathered up and the helicopter returns to fly you back to Salinas. The hunts are a flat rate of $1,300, including everything once you reach Salinas. You can take two animals—two pigs or, during the A-Zone deer season, a pig and a deer or two deer. Even though this is technically a public-land hunt, it's more like hunting private land, and success is high. For the past three years, Massolo's clients have enjoyed 70 to 80 percent success. Hog hunting is year round.

Hog Wild/Mark Williams Guide Service
P.O. Box 1497, King City, CA 93930
831-385-6321
e-mail: hogwild@redshift.com

Mark Williams offers guided pig hunts on six ranches totaling more than 50,000 acres, located in the prime hog areas of Monterey and San Benito counties east and west of King City. Williams has been guiding since 1972 and knows the country better than most of us do our own backyards. The hunting is spot-and-stalk, and much of it, particularly from early spring until early fall, focuses on the barley fields, which are surrounded by chaparral brush and oak savanna. Pigs are attracted to this readily available food source, and their movements become predictable. Williams offers two-day guided hunts for $450. Lodging and meals can be arranged for an additional fee. Over the years, Hog Wild clients have enjoyed 90-plus percent success. The ranches support high-density hog populations, including quality boars. Williams also offers turkey, deer, and upland bird hunting in season.

Las Viboras Wild Boar Hunts
54 Comstock Rd., #B, Hollister, CA 95023
831-637-7770

Ed Sparling hosts guided hog hunts on his 6,500-acre cattle ranch in San Benito County twelve miles northeast of Hollister. The habitat is rolling hills covered with oak woodland and annual grassland. There is very little brush and no farming. Sparling hunts with dogs between 1 November and 30 April when the weather is cool. The dogs will find pigs, and his clients take home the bacon on virtually every hunt. Day hunts are $200, plus an additional $200 when a pig is harvested. Most of his hunters are from the San Francisco Bay Area, only a two-hour drive away. The nearest accommodations and restaurants are in Hollister.

Miller Brothers Expeditions
70502 Vineyard Canyon Rd., San Miguel, CA 93451
805-463-2475 or 805-459-5883

Roger Miller conducts hunts on a 6,000-acre ranch just outside Parkfield where the habitat is typical central-coast oak woodlands, chaparral, and annual grassland, along with cultivated barley and grape vineyards. This combination of native cover and cultivated crops not only supports good pig populations but also produces good-size hogs. Meat pigs average 150 pounds and trophy boars 250 (a few top 300). Miller offers spot-and-stalk hunting only, year-round. Some of the best of it is from late May through late August when the barley and grapes are ripening. Hunter success averages 90 percent or better. Miller offers two-day hunts for $500. The rate does not include accommodations, but a cabin that sleeps up to seven and has cooking facilities is available on the ranch for $50 a night per group. Other hunters prefer to stay at the Parkfield Inn only a mile away. Miller Brothers also offers dove, quail, and turkey hunting in season.

Mustang Guide Service
P.O. Box 2144, King City, CA 93930
831-386-9027

Frank Morasci has owned and operated Mustang Guide Service for fifteen years and works thirteen ranches totaling about 150,000 acres. With that many acres, Morasci seldom takes a client to a "dry hole." The ranches are within a thirty-mile radius of King City in the heart of wild-hog country. The habitat varies from rolling oak savanna to brushy draws and includes some dryland barley and grape vineyards. About 75 percent of the 100 to 150 hogs his clients bag annually (95 percent success rate) are taken by spot-and-stalk hunting, the remainder using dogs. When the hunting gets tough, dogs are often the difference between success and failure. Hunts are held all year. Morasci offers two-day hunts for $400, and there is no kill fee. The ratio of meat hogs to trophy boars is about fifteen to one. Hunters generally stay in King City, where there are numerous motels and restaurants.

Nessen Schmidt Guide Service
Oasis Rd., Box 105, King City, CA 93930
831-385-1335

With eleven ranches and a total of 180,000 acres leased, Nessen Schmidt is one of the largest operators on the central coast. He also has stood the test of time, having logged nearly thirty years in the guide business. The ranches he hunts are roughly within twenty-five miles of King City in prime hog country—rolling hills covered with oak woodland, brush, annual grassland, and dryland barley. He offers both spot-and-stalk and hunting with dogs. About 70 percent of the hogs are taken by spot-and-stalk, and those hunters see about 90 percent success; the dog hunts virtually always produce results.

Schmidt hunts all year and, like many other guides, finds the pigs most concentrated from late May through September, when they frequent the barley fields. Schmidt takes about twenty meat hogs for every trophy boar. Two-day hunts are $400, with no additional fee for a meat hog. A trophy boar with tusks longer than two inches will cost you an additional $200. Clients stay in King City, where Schmidt recommends the hunter-friendly Keffer's Motel. Schmidt also guides for wild turkeys and free-ranging exotic sheep.

Panoche Valley Game Ranch
7197 W. Carmellia, Dos Palos, CA 93620
209-601-1646 or 209-613-4630
email: czuniga93635@yahoo.com

The Hennagans have owned this ranch for five generations. Currently, Chip Hennagan guides on a 3,500-acre property thirty miles southeast of Hollister in San Benito County. The habitat is typical of the dryer east side of the coast range—annual grass, scattered oaks, and plenty of brush and rugged terrain. Between September and May, Hennagan offers guided hunts with dogs. During June, July, and August he allows trespass hunts—he points you in the right direction, then it's up to you. Success on the dog hunts runs 95 percent while hunters on their own score about 50 percent of the time. The property holds plenty of meat hogs and a few trophy boars. Hennagan charges $250 a day for the dog hunts and $150 a day for the unguided hunts with no kill fee. Hunters stay in Hollister or along Interstate 5. Wild turkeys, deer, and upland birds can be hunted in season.

Redfern Ranch
4165 Canada Rd., Gilroy, CA 95020
831-634-1866 or 408-842-4602

Redfern is a 4,200-acre cattle operation about five miles east of Gilroy in Santa Clara County. The hunting program is only three years old and is run by Mark Klassen. The habitat is typical coastal range oak savanna, annual grass, and chaparral. Hunting is always open, and though Redfern's track record is limited, it has enjoyed 95-plus percent success. The hunting is spot-and-stalk and good all year; it's the most challenging during winter months. The targets are primarily meat animals along with a few trophies. One-day hunts are $400; two-day hunts with accommodations are $650.

This bow hunter is walking up on a pig shot only a few minutes earlier. Always approach a hog with caution and keep your weapon ready until you know the animal is dead. There is more than one story of hunters walking up to a dead hog only to have it stand up and run away!

Rock Springs Ranch
11000 Old Hernandez Rd., Paicines, CA 95043
800-209-5175; fax 831-385-5270
Web site: www.rockspringsranch.com

Few hog-hunting places are as upscale as Rock Springs Ranch. It's a well-known bird-hunting (California quail, doves, preserve pheasants, chukars, bobwhites) operation that also offers wild hogs and deer. This 19,000-acre ranch, in operation since 1994, is located thirty miles northeast of King City. The habitat, oak woodland and chaparral ranging from 1,500 to 4,000 feet in elevation, supports a thriving population of hogs.

There are two pig-hunting programs. In May-June and August-September, the ranch offers guided hunts (Wednesday to Friday or Friday to Sunday) that include two hunting days, three nights' accommodations, and meals for $800. During the preserve bird season from October to April, hog hunting can be an add-on to the bird hunts. A one-day bird hunt including meals and accommodations is $800. Pigs can be hunted in the afternoon for no additional cost, but if you take one, there is a $450 fee. The hunting is spot-and-stalk, and success is around 90 percent for meat hogs and 25 to 30 percent for big boars. Six guides are available. The accommodations are in a first-class 8,500-square-foot lodge, and the quality of the food is more like an upscale restaurant than a hunting lodge.

Santa Lucia Outfitters
100 Old Stage Rd., Salinas, CA 93908
831-444-7100

Al and Rhena Agostini have been hunting pigs on their 1,500-acre ranch for ten years. The ranch, located about ten miles north of Salinas in San Benito County, has rolling hills dominated by oak savanna and chamise brush. Pig hunts are held from early January to mid-April, when the hogs tend to be out in the open rooting for acorns and bulbs. The hunts are spot-and-stalk, and over the years clients have enjoyed 80-plus-percent success. Most of the meat hogs run 125 to 150 pounds, the trophy boars 250 to 300 pounds. Clients here take one trophy boar for every ten meat hogs. Agostini keeps very close track of the big boars and offers hunts specifically for them.

Day hunts are a flat $450 for a meat hog and $750 for a trophy boar. The price does not include meals or lodging. Hunters stay in Salinas and drive to the ranch early in the morning of the hunt. Santa Lucia Outfitters specialize in horseback trips into the Ventana and Silver Peak wilderness areas for deer and turkeys. They also offer a few horseback trips into the wilderness for wild pigs.

S. Q. Guide Service
Box 5, Bitterwater Rd., King City, CA 93930
831-385-0154

Rick Eskue has been guiding on two ranches (23,000 and 1,000 acres) fifteen miles east of King City off Highway 25 for five years. The ranches are dominated by rolling hills covered with oak woodland, annual grassland, chamise brush, and some dryland barley. The hunting is spot-and-stalk, and hunter success is 95 percent. Five or six quality boars are killed out of every one hundred animals harvested. You can hunt all year, but it's best from May through September. Eskue offers two-day weekend-only hunts for a flat rate of $400. Accommodations in a double-wide trailer are available for $25 per person per night. Bring your own food, water, and bedding.

T-Bone's Guide Service
48460 Airline Highway, King City, CA 93930
831-385-5009

Brian Palmer, better known as T-bone, operates on four ranches totaling 25,000 acres, about fifteen miles east of King City off Highway 25 in both Monterey and San Benito counties. The habitat is typical: oak woodland, grass, and brush plus dryland barley. While Palmer has been guiding for twenty-five years, he has operated the guide service for the past six seasons. The spot-and-stalk hunting is best from May through September. In years when there is a good acorn crop, the hogs concentrate in the oak woodlands, and the hunting holds up through the fall and winter. Hunter success has been 85 to 90 percent in recent years. T-bone charges $400 for a two-day hunt, and there is no trophy fee for a large boar. Bunkhouse-style accommodations are available for $25 a day per person for the two-day hunt. Clients looking for a bit more comfort drive fifteen miles to King City.

Tom Willoughby Outfitter and Guide Service
P.O. Box 1467, King City, CA 93930
831-385-3003

Willoughby is one of the senior statesmen of the central-California hog-hunting business, having guided in Monterey County for nearly twenty-five years. Currently, he leases eight ranches that cover about 110,000 acres total. They are between King City and Paso Robles, and the habitat is oak woodland, annual grassland, chamise brush, and dryland barley. Willoughby told me that due to the low prices the ranchers have been getting for grain, the acres planted to barley have declined in recent years. About 75 percent of his hunters prefer spot-and-stalk hunting, with some of the most consistent action occurring from late spring to late summer when the barley is ripening. During the winter, the pigs are more scattered and he has a tendency to use dogs more. Meat hogs average 150 pounds, and the big boars go from 225 pounds to the rare 350-pound monster. Willoughby offers two-day hunts for a flat rate of $400 and guarantees he will get you within shooting range of a pig. The rest is up to you. Overall, his rifle hunters have enjoyed 95 percent success. Hunters stay in either King City or Paso Robles.

Twisselman Outfitters
7685 Cattle Dr., Santa Margarita, CA 93453
805-475-2437
Web site: www.twisselmanoutfitters.com

About forty miles east of Santa Margarita off Highway 58, Noland and Stacey Twisselman and brother Andrew operate Twisselman Outfitters. They hunt on an 80,000-acre ranch in San Luis and Kern counties. They have been guiding for more than ten years and have a good client base. The habitat is oak woodland, annual grassland, brush, and dryland barley. Spot-and-stalk hunters take one trophy boar for every twelve to fifteen meat hogs. Over the years, hunter success has averaged 95 percent, and hunts are held all yearlong. Two-day packages include accommodations in a fully equipped bunkhouse (bring your own food). Meat hogs are $475 and trophy boars $575. Upland bird and tule elk hunts are also available.

Wild Thang Hunting Adventures
P.O. Box 452, Shandon, CA 93461
805-239-9494
Web site: www.wildthanghunting.com

This is a booking agency that can arrange pig hunts on more than 100,000 acres of private ranch land in the central-coast region. Most of the guides/outfitters Wild Thang represents also book directly with hunters and are mentioned individually in these pages. However, owner-operator Mark Sawdey does represent one guide who has not been mentioned—Clint White, who guides on two ranches totaling about 10,000 acres east of Paso Robles in the Shandon/Parkfield area. The habitat is much the same as most other ranches on the central coast. The hunting is mostly spot-and-stalk, but dogs are occasionally used to root hogs out of the brush. Hunting is available year-round, and the barley season always delivers solid action. Hunting success is 95-plus percent. Two-day hunts booked by Wild Thang and guided by White are a flat rate of $500 for meat hogs and $650 for trophy boars. Hunters camp on the ranch or drive to Paso Robles. Wild Thang also books deer, turkey, upland bird, and varmint hunts on several ranches in the central-coast region.

Work's Wildlife Management
77502 Hog Canyon Rd., San Miguel, CA 93451
805-467-3262
Web site: www.pig-hunt.com

With just under 100,000 acres leased on two ranches, Work's Wildlife Management, owned and operated by Bert Claassen, is one of the larger operators on the central coast. Bert, who has been guiding since the late 1970s, operates on the 85,000-acre Jack Ranch, three miles south of Parkfield, and the 12,000-acre Work Ranch, eight miles southwest of Parkfield. Both properties are in southern Monterey County. The varied habitat ranges from draws dominated by chaparral to rolling hills where oak savanna is the primary vegetation. Cattle grazing is the main use for the land. Both ranches incorporate agriculture into their operations. The Jack Ranch is primarily alfalfa and row crops while the Work Ranch grows barley. The Work Ranch has offered pig hunts for years, but the Jack Ranch has been open to guided hunts only since January 2000. Each year, Claassen's clients take about 300 wild hogs on the two ranches combined. The hunting is spot-and-stalk, open all year, and virtually every hunter gets a shot. Hunting is productive all year, but there are peak times when plenty of animals are around to size up. On the Jack Ranch, it's from April to July, when the hogs come out of the brush to root in the hay fields. On the Work Ranch, it coincides with the maturation of the barley crop— May to August. In the fall, action shifts to the oak woodlands, where the hogs feed on acorns. The diet of hay, barley, and acorns grows meat hogs of 150 to 175 pounds and husky boars of 250 to 300 pounds.

Work's Wildlife Management offers two-day hunts on both ranches. On the Jack Ranch, the rate is $500 for a meat hog and $600 for a trophy. An additional pig is $200. Hunters can stay in a single-wide trailer that sleeps eight for no additional cost, or go into town and stay at the Parkfield Inn and eat at a local café. On the Work Ranch, the price is $325 for a two-day hunt, with an additional $225 if you kill a pig (a big boar or meat hog); room and board is included.

San Joaquin Valley/Foothills

B & B Outfitters and Guide Service
813 Coastal Ct., Los Banos, CA 93635
209-827-6193
e-mail: winchester@cell2000.net

Bill Marchese has been hunting on his 1,100-acre family ranch for years. Four years ago he began offering guided hunts on this Merced County property, located southwest of the junction of Interstate 5 and Highway 152 near Los Banos. The habitat is characteristic of the west-side valley foothills—scattered oaks, annual grassland, juniper, and brush. The hunting is spot-and-stalk, and there is a nice mix of meat hogs and trophy boars. Hunter success has averaged about 80 percent. Marchese offers hunts between January and mid-May, when he feels the pigs are in the best condition. The price of a one-day hunt that includes cabin accommodations on the ranch and meals is $300, and a two-day hunt is $350. There is an additional kill fee of $100 for a meat hog and $150 for a trophy boar with tusks longer than two inches. Clients must have a 4x4 vehicle and use it when hunting on the ranch.

Blue Ridge Guide Service
46438 Blue Ridge Dr., Springville, CA 93265
559-539-5102 fax 559-539-2572
e-mail: bluridge@inreach.com

Bill Sweetser has owned and operated Blue Ridge for twenty-seven years. He guides in two areas. His main area is west of Springville off Highway 190 in the Sierra foothills of Tulare County. He has 5,000 acres leased on two ranches, and spot-and-stalk is the primary method. Most of the area is annual grassland and oak woodland. Sweetser offers day hunts for $150 a hunter, plus a kill fee of $400. He emphasizes trophy boars, and most of his clients come for the big boys. A typical mature boar will weigh about 250 pounds and carry two- to three-inch tusks. The hunting is most consistent in spring and early summer, when the hogs feed on green grass and forage out in the open. Hunters generally stay at the Springville Inn or in Porterville. Food and lodging are not included in the day rate.

Sweetser's second area is a 1,500-acre ranch near Paso Robles. Though relatively small, it supports high hog populations. A good percentage of the ranch is devoted to dryland barley and safflower surrounded by typical coastal brush habitat. The big draw here is the food provided by the grain crops. Hunters wait in ambush for the pigs to move out of the brush and into open feeding areas. Hunting is particularly good in late spring, when the barley is in the "dough" stage. The boars here get big and can weigh up to 400 pounds—a direct result of the abundant groceries. Prices are the same as for the Tulare County ranch, and you're on your own for food and lodging. Sweetser also guides for deer, turkeys, black bears, and predators.

Cedar Canyon Outdoor Adventures
3 Blackburn Ct., Paso Robles, CA 93446
805-238-6557

Cedar Canyon operates on a 26,000-acre working cattle ranch fifty miles east of Paso Robles off Highway 46 in Kern County. Elevation is 3,000 feet in the Temblor Range, and the cover is chaparral brush, annual grass, juniper, and scattered oaks. Jim Davis, head guide, offers spot-and-stalk hunting year-round on weekends only, and hunting success is 95 percent. Davis told me that most of the hogs are meat animals in the 125- to 160-pound range. One-day hunts are $250 plus a $200 kill fee (meat pig or trophy boar). Clients stay in Paso Robles or can rent a cabin that sleeps up to six for $100 a night. Bring your own food and bedding. Cedar Canyon also offers hunts for tule elk and quail.

Hogs Wild
P.O. Box 355, Coalinga, CA 93210
559-935-5788

Larry Greve owns and operates Hogs Wild and has been in the guiding business for more than twenty-five years. He leases two ranches totaling 14,000 acres and one 2,000-acre ranch that is restricted to bowhunting. All three properties are west of Coalinga off Highway 198. The habitat is typical of the east slope of the coast range—annual grass, oak savanna, and brush along with some barley and pastures. The hunting is spot-and-stalk in two different programs—guided rifle hunts and semiguided archery hunts. The bow hunts include an orientation, and Greve will help you pack out your hog, but when hunting, you're on your own. Rifle hunters always get a shot here, and success is in the 95 percent range; the semiguided bow hunters score about 40 percent of the time. While he hunts all year, Greve likes the months of May, June, and July, when pigs are feeding in the barley fields and are tied to water. The properties all produce a good mix of meat pigs and trophy boars.

Two-day guided rifle hunts are $425, and the semiguided archery hunts are $275. Lodging is not included, but there are camping areas on the ranches as well as cabins for $10 a person per night. Bring your own food, water, and bedding. Motels are available in Coalinga.

Mike Berry's Guide Service
2312 Castro Lane, Bakersfield, CA 93304
661-397-7008

Mike Berry hunts on two ranches totaling 6,000 acres, plus 100,000 acres of BLM ground on the east side of the San Joaquin Valley in the Sierra foothills, about twenty-five miles east of Bakersfield in Kern County. He has been guiding for twenty-eight years and has operated on these ranches for five years. The habitat is oak woodland, brush, and annual grass. You can hunt all year here, with the most productive period being from March through late May, when the weather is mild and the pigs are active. In the summer the hogs are hunted near water but are active for only a short period very early and late in the day. The hunting is spot-and-stalk, and success averages 95 percent. Both meat hogs and trophy boars are available. One-day hunts cost $375. Hunters can stay in a bunkhouse on the ranch (bring your own food) or stay in Bakersfield. Berry also offers deer, bear, bobcat, and exotic sheep and goat hunts.

Turk Station Lodge
P.O. Box 416, Coalinga, CA 93210
559-935-1902
Web site: www.turkstationlodge.com

Located minutes from Interstate 5 and just south of Highway 198 near Coalinga, Turk Station is one of the newer and more upscale hog-hunting operations in California. Owned and operated by Ross Allen, it has been in business since 1999 as a pheasant-hunting preserve. In 2001, hog hunting was added. The base of operations is Turk Station Lodge, a 1910 plantation-style home that has been completely transformed into a hunting lodge. The hog hunts are on two ranches totaling about 20,000 acres near Coalinga in Fresno County, on a 7,000-acre ranch between Hollister and King City in San Benito County, and on a 10,000-acre ranch in the Carmel Valley southeast of Monterey. The hunting is spot-and-stalk, and hunter success was 90 percent in the operation's first year out. All the properties offer a nice mix of meat hogs and trophy boars. Hunting is offered year-round.

There are several different hog packages. The Carmel Valley option is a day hunt that includes guide service and lunch. Fees are $450 a person for two hunters, $550 for single hunters, and $650 for bow hunters. The San Benito County ranch is available as a guided day hunt for $300 per hunter (minimum of two hunters) plus a $150 kill fee. The Coalinga ranch hunts are sold as three-day/two-night packages that include hunting services, lodging in Turk Station Lodge, and quality meals. The price is $750 a hunter in parties of two or more, $850 for a single, $950 for bow hunters. There is no additional kill fee, and a second pig can be taken for $200. Finally, there is a hog/bird package for four days and three nights that includes hog hunting and up to three days of shooting preserve pheasants, bobwhites, and chukars. The all-inclusive price is $1,000 a person in parties of two or more or $1,200 for a single. A second pig is an additional $200, and nonshooting guests pay $135 a night. These combo hunts are available 1 October to 1 April. The preserve bird hunts can be booked by the day (with or without lodging) as well as in multi-day packages. The preserve bird season is 1 September to 1 May. Preserve-bird day rates start at $375. An afternoon hog hunt can be added to a bird shoot for $200 plus a $200 kill fee. Dove and California quail hunts are available in season.

Southern California

Big Country Outfitters
1882 E. Larch St., Simi, CA 93065
805-584-6283

Since 1998, Don Smith has operated Big Country Outfitters for archers only. He hunts on the Tejon Ranch, where 50,000 acres have been dedicated to bow hunters. The habitat is one-third bottomland and riparian areas along watercourses that are relatively flat, and two-thirds hilly to steep terrain dominated by brush, annual grassland, and oak woodland. Smith offers semiguided hunts in which he takes the archers out in the morning, drops them off, and then picks them up at noon, repeating the process in the afternoon. If you kill a pig, he will help you get it out. The semiguided hunts include accommodations in a cabin (bring your own food). Success on the semiguided hunts runs about 35 percent. Smith also offers fully guided hunts that include food and cabin accommodations.

Hunter success on these is 80 to 90 percent. The semiguided hunts are priced at $425 and the guided hunts at $625. There is no additional kill fee, and a second pig can be taken for $225. Both programs start at noon Friday and run until Sunday noon. Smith offers hunts between November and August.

Bighorn Ranch
16702 Darkwood Dr., Riverside, CA 92506
909-789-4690

Bighorn is the only high-fenced property I could locate in California that offers hog hunting. Some hunters shy away from fenced operations while others welcome them. Owners Jim and Chuck Wagner have operated since the mid-1980s, hunting wild hogs, feral goats, and exotic sheep in a fenced 800-acre ranch about ten miles west of Beaumont in Riverside County. The terrain is dominated by rolling hills, and the habitat is a mixture of annual grassland and brush with a few oak trees. The hunting is spot-and-stalk, and hunter success is 99 percent. Hunters are provided a map of the ranch, then turned loose to hunt on their own. Once an animal is down, they will help you get it out. The cost for a one-day hunt is $290, with no additional kill fee. Most of the hogs are meat animals from 100 to 175 pounds; a few boars go 300 pounds.

Tejon Ranch
P.O. Box 1000, Lebec, CA 93243
661-663-4208
Web site: www.tejonranch.com

Not only is the Tejon one of the few places in southern California where you can hunt wild hogs, it is one of the largest ranches in California. Founded in 1843, it covers 270,000 acres and is a diversified real-estate development and agribusiness company. It's sixty miles north of Los Angeles and thirty miles south of Bakersfield along Interstate 5 near Lebec in Kern County. This huge expanse of land encompasses much of the Tehachapi Mountains and includes pine and fir forests at elevations up to 7,000 feet northeast of Gorman, as well as grape vineyards near sea level at the foot of the Tehachapis southeast of Wheeler Ridge. In addition to farming, cattle, and real estate, the Tejon has a resource management program that includes hunting for a wide variety of species from Rocky Mountain elk and deer to varmints and upland gamebirds.

Wild hogs are a top draw here. The Tejon offers two-day hog hunts for $650 per hunter, which includes all hunting services, accommodations, and meals. Hunters are housed in a cabin with a bunkroom, two double-occupancy rooms, and a bathroom down the hall. The hunting is spot-and-stalk and can occur at the edge of agricultural fields, in pristine oak woodlands, in dense brush, or in anything between. Every hunter gets a shot, and few go home empty-handed. The Tejon Ranch also offers a unique unguided hunting opportunity. Each year, six or seven weekend-access-only hunts, dubbed Pig-O-Ramas, allow hunters to enter on Friday at noon and hunt on their own until Sunday evening for a flat rate of $300. Hunters are assigned to one of three very large areas, and the number in each area is limited. The hunter hanging the heaviest field-dressed hog at the end of the weekend in each of the three areas scores $500 in prize money.

Chapter 5

After the Hunt

Prehunt preparations and then the hunt itself are the primary components of the overall experience. However, don't sell short what happens after you have an animal down. Psychologists tell us that each personal experience can be divided into three parts. One-third is the anticipation value—looking forward to the hunt, setting it up, getting your gear ready, buying new equipment, and traveling to the hunt area. Another one-third is the participation value—the hunt itself, the thrill of the chase, finding a huge boar and stalking it, and putting the animal down. The final one-third is the reflection value, or how you look back on the experience and what happens after the hunt: telling your buddies about the hunt, looking at photos of you with your trophy, savoring a barbecued wild-hog backstrap. All three parts make up the complete experience. This chapter delves into the reflection segments of the experience.

Photographing the Harvest

Most hunters take at least a few snapshots of the game they kill. The photos are for personal enjoyment later and help establish bragging rights with the guys back home. Taking photos can be accomplished with anything from a disposable camera to a more sophisticated 35mm single-lens-reflex model. Some of the better point-and-shoot cameras come with built-in timers, a telephoto lens, and flash. These are probably the best buys for the money— they are light, you can get a shot of you and your trophy even if you're alone, and the flash ensures decent shots even on a cloudy day or at night.

Put your camera in a waterproof plastic Ziplock bag and keep it in your pack, where it won't get damaged. Don't forget extra film. Most people shoot print film of 100 ASA or 200 ASA, the proper film speeds for most situations. You can use 400 ASA on overcast days, but the shots will be grainier in appearance than with 100 or 200. In the case of slides, most professional photographers use 100 ASA film.

Whatever camera and film you use, there are several things you should take into account. There's a reason I put the photography section of the chapter before field dressing and care of the meat. The biggest photo mistake most hunters make is taking the shots after the animal has been gutted. Many well-focused and well-lighted hunting photos are ruined by a gut pile in the background, a gaping body cavity, or a hunter with blood up to his armpits. I'm not squeamish and neither are most hunters, but blood and gore should not be shown prominently in your photos!

In Europe, respect for the kill is a prime element in the presentation of game for others to see. A wild boar is often brought back whole to the hunting lodge so it can be cleaned up and presented to other hunters. Most magazine editors here in the U.S. do publish "hero" shots—photos of hunters with dead game. However, if such shots are not presented in what might be considered an "antiseptic" manner, they generally do not get published.

Take photos as soon as possible after the kill. For one thing, you want to get the picture taking over with and move on to the field-dressing stage. Second, the animal will be easier to move and position for photos before rigor mortis sets in. In setting up for photos, first consider the location of the animal and whether you want to photograph it there. The place where a pig expires is seldom the best location for photos. It may be in heavy shade, on a steep sidehill, or in the middle of a brushpile. More often than not, I move the animal at least a few yards. If another person is with you, he can take photos of you and your hog and help move the animal to a better spot. Drag animals out of the brush into the open or to a place where the background is better—a skyline, for instance. Also consider the direction of the light. It's always better to photograph the animal in direct light, so put the sun behind the photographer and in your face when you're next to the pig. If you wear a hat, take it off or tilt it back to get some light on your face. How many pictures have you seen where the face is so shaded by the bill of a hat that the person's mug is unrecognizable? Don't photograph directly into the sun.

On overcast days, light direction may be difficult to determine. In that case, you can photograph from any angle, and if your camera has a built-in flash, use it. Also make sure the person taking the photos pays attention to his shadow and doesn't allow it to show in the photo. This is easily accomplished by having the cameraman move around until his shadow falls outside the picture.

If there's a gaping wound or excessive blood on one side, turn the animal around and photograph its good side. I always bring several rags and some water with me. Once the animal has been positioned for the photo, I do my best to wipe the blood from the nostrils and mouth and any other gory location. Make sure the tongue isn't hanging out. Use water sparingly, for it can make its own mess. Take close-up shots as well as wider shots that show the habitat. Don't just photograph you and the animal; take some shots of the countryside and you walking up to the hog. Remember, photos are like bullets—they are cheap and a tiny portion of the expense involved in taking a wild hog. Tasteful photos complement the harvest, compliment the hunter, and serve as an integral part of the reflection value of the hunt.

Field Dressing and Caring for Meat

Many people consider a 125-pound pig one of the best eating of all wild game animals. However, it must be taken care of properly in the field. The meat is darker than domestic pork, and the flavor is more robust while still maintaining the mild taste characteristic of pork. In contrast, a 300-pound boar can be tough as nails, and everything on it but the tenderloin is best made into sausage or jerky. Some will take exception to this statement, and butcher a large boar as they would a meat hog. My answer? Let your palate be your guide!

As with other big game, the cleaner the meat is kept and the quicker it's cooled, the better it will taste. The goal of field dressing and the key to good-tasting wild pork is to transform a large, warm animal into a cool, clean carcass as soon as possible. Even in relatively cool weather, it is wise to gut an animal in the first hour after it has expired. Once the tag has been attached

The warmer the weather, the quicker the carcass should be skinned to promote the cooling process and avoid spoilage. The most common and easiest method is to hang the carcass by the hindquarters. More and more hunters are using rubber or surgical gloves to keep their hands clean and to keep out bacteria that might enter a cut or scratch.

and the photos taken, it's time to get dirty. As mentioned in an earlier chapter, many hunters bring rubber or surgical gloves to keep their hands clean and to keep out bacteria that might enter a cut or scratch.

Position the animal so its hindquarters are downhill. This will aid in the removal of the entrails later. Make an incision around the anus to separate the lower end of the intestine from the carcass. Open the body cavity by making an incision from the anus along the centerline of the belly toward the throat. Go around the genitals, and if you plan on mounting the head, stop at the breastbone. Make sure you are cutting only through the hide and skin, not into the entrails themselves. Try always to cut away from you to avoid injury. Once the incision from anus to breastbone or throat is completed, reach in and cut away the diaphragm that is connected to the spine. By now the entrails should be at least partially out of the cavity. Continue to cut away any connective tissue that holds the entrails to the rib cage, taking care not to cut the intestines or stomach. Reach in and sever the windpipe, pull down, and everything should come out of the cavity. Handle the bladder carefully—you don't want to get urine on the meat. Cut away bloodshot meat, and wipe out the body cavity with a damp rag. If you want to take the dressing chore a step farther, a meat saw will be necessary to split the breastbone. As you saw through the bone, try not to dig the saw into the back of the chest cavity.

If you are going to leave the field-dressed carcass and return for it later, prop the cavity open with a stick to increase cooling, and make sure it is in the shade. Don't take forever to return; don't leave the carcass out overnight, or the coyotes, bears, and even other wild hogs might take care of it for you. If you can, hoist it up into a tree with the body propped open—it will cool even quicker and be more difficult for scavengers to reach.

Dragging and packframes are the most frequently used methods of moving hogs. You may be able to drive a pickup or ATV to the animal and load it whole. Other situations will require moving the animal some distance. Lots of pigs have been dragged merely by holding onto the front legs and pulling. Some hunters use a harness that allows you to drag the animal with your torso instead of your arms. I like wheeled game carriers to get animals out of the field.

Game carts or carriers with wheels take the strain out of transporting game. Here Scott Currier and the author haul out a wild hog on a one-wheel game cart. (Photo by Kelly Kramer)

However, the packframe is the most frequently used method of moving a hog any distance. If the size of the hog allows it, you can put the whole animal in the packframe bag or lash it directly to the frame. Larger hogs will have to be cut in half or quartered. And if you are a long way from the vehicle, you may have to bone out the meat.

Skinning can take place either at the kill site or after the pig has been gutted and moved to a more convenient location. The warmer the weather, the quicker the carcass should be skinned, to promote the cooling process and prevent spoilage. The easiest prep for the skinning chore is to hang the carcass by the hindquarters. Some hunters cut or saw off the legs at the knee joint, but because hogs have such short legs, you may not want to do so. A gambrel to separate the legs and hold them in place is handy but not a requirement.

First, cut through the skin around each leg near the hock. Hold the blade in such a way that you don't cut into the meat. Then, starting from inside the hind leg, make a cut that reaches the cut around the knee. Start pulling the hide downward from the top of the leg, cutting it free where necessary. Cut through the tail where it joins the body. Do the same on the other side, continually pulling the hide down until you get near the front legs. Make a cut around each front leg at the knee, then cut the hide down each front leg to the centerline, continuing to pull down. Work the hide over the shoulders and to the neck, then cut it off just above the head. Cut the head off at a vertebra joint or leave it on.

If you plan to hang the skinned carcass outside, put it in a commercially made deer bag or a muslin bag and make sure it's closed properly. The bag will allow air to circulate but keep flies off the meat. If the weather is warm, try to get the carcass to a cool box or a butcher right away. If the temperature is 40 to 50 degrees, you can hang the carcass for a day or two; if it's 30 to 40 degrees, you can hang it for several days.

Larger boars are often skinned using the strip method. Hang the hog by the head, and cut through the skin around the neck. With a sharp knife, perhaps a carpet knife, make cuts perpendicular to the neck, down the length of the body, six inches apart. Peel each resulting strip down off the carcass, cutting the hide away where necessary.

If you'll have to transport the carcass a long distance from your hunting location to where it will be processed, it's wise to have it skinned and thoroughly cooled down first. A good way to keep the carcass cool is to wrap it in an old sleeping bag or quilt and cover it with a tarp. Try to keep it out of direct sunlight.

If you've flown to the hunting area, taking meat home can pose a problem. If there's time, have the meat cut, wrapped, and frozen, pack it in an ice chest, and check it as baggage. Be sure the chest does not exceed seventy pounds—the standard airline weight limit for a single package or bag. There may be an extra charge for excess baggage. You cannot use ice—dry or wet—but frozen meat won't thaw for at least twenty-four hours. On short flights, I've checked as baggage meat that was chilled, placed in two garbage bags, then put in a duffel bag.

Caping and Taxidermy

If you want a shoulder mount, you must cape the animal properly. A mount requires that in field dressing the hog, you open the body cavity only as far as the breastbone. To remove the cape, first cut all the way around the body behind the front legs—this will give the taxidermist plenty of hide to work with. Next, cut from the breastbone down the backside of each front leg to the knee, then cut around the leg at the knee. Peel the hide off the hog as you would a sock. When you get to the base of the skull, cut through the neck to the vertebrae just below the skull and sever at a joint. You'll have to use a saw on the big boars. If you know what you are doing, you can remove the hide from the skull, using special care when working around the eyes, ears, and mouth. If you don't, I strongly suggest letting your taxidermist do that chore. If you can't get the cape to the taxidermist quickly, freeze it or apply a generous amount of salt to the skinned side. Don't skimp on the salt—use three to five pounds. Once the salt is applied, wrap the cape up, put it in a plastic bag, and store it in a cool place. In cool weather it will hold for a couple of days.

Select a taxidermist who is familiar with mounting wild pigs (bypass, for example, a shop that mounts mostly birds). Expect to pay $500 to $800 for a shoulder mount and $1,500 to $2,000 for a full body mount. Big boars with big tusks make the most impressive trophies, but a skilled taxidermist can make a smaller animal look quite impressive. Most people like to mount black boars in the open-mouth pose.

Processing Meat

OK, let's assume the carcass has been properly cared for in the field and you have transported it home. Processing the meat is the next step. There are two ways to go about it—cut and wrap it yourself or take it to a commercial processing establishment for butchering. Lots of hunters have learned how to butcher their own meat: It's less expensive, you get the cuts you prefer, and you don't risk having your hog intentionally or unintentionally switched with someone else's. Butchering requires a couple of sharp knives, a sharpening stone, bowls to hold the meat until it's wrapped, freezer paper, tape, and a permanent marking pen. A 150-pound meat pig will yield fifty to sixty pounds of boned-out meat.

First, remove the tenderloins from the inside top of the body cavity along the backbone. This is the filet mignon—the tenderest cut. Leave it in one or two pieces, or cut it crosswise into steaks. Next, remove the backstrap from the top of the back and cut it into steaks. I always cut the steaks the same thickness for uniform cooking, and package tenderloin steaks together and backstrap steaks together. Double-wrap the steaks in freezer paper, and indicate the cut and date on the package with a marking pen. Each package should contain an amount that will serve as a meal for your family.

The next step depends on how much precision you want to apply to the butchering. Some hunters have learned to make the cuts you would find in a butcher shop; others cut the choice steaks and roasts off the bone and turn the rest into stewmeat, sausage, or burger. The choice is yours, and the more times you do your own butchering, the better you will get at it. To make hamburger or sausage, you will need a grinder, and because wild pork is lean, you might want to add 10 percent pork suet to the burger. Small grinders can be purchased through outdoor catalogs like Cabela's. Once the meat is cut and wrapped, freeze it as soon as possible. If the meat has been packaged properly, it should last up to a year.

The other option—a far simpler one—is to deliver the carcass (preferably cooled and skinned) to a butcher. Meat processors will skin the carcass for you, at an additional charge. Be sure to tell the butcher the type of cuts you want, the size of the packages (i.e., for four people, one pound of sausage, etc.), the type of sausage you want, and whether you want the hams smoked. With meat pigs, I always get the hams smoked, and have found them excellent. They are a bit more robust than domestic ham and similar to prosciutto (Italian ham). Smoking the hams and making sausage will add to the basic cut-and-wrap price.

In recent years it has become increasingly difficult to find meat processors/butchers who will accept wild game and do a good job of butchering it. Here are several reputable butchers in each of the primary pig-hunting regions as well as the San Francisco Bay and Los Angeles/Orange County areas. This information is provided as a service, not as an endorsement of each operation.

Sacramento Valley and the Foothills

Chico Locker and Sausage Co., 196 E. 14th St., Chico, CA 95928; 530-343-7370.

Thayer's Custom Butchering, 19855B So. Main St., Cottonwood, CA 96022; 530-347-5271.

Clear Creek Grocery and Locker, 7036 Westside Rd., Redding, CA 96001; 530-246-9044.

North Coast

Eureka Wholesale Meats, 226 G St., Eureka, CA 95501; 707-443-5659.

The Superette Market, 6195 North State St., Calpella, CA 95418; 707-485-8605.

Central Coast

Cynnie O'Connor Game Processor, 19A Bitterwater Rd., King City, CA 93930; 831-385-6906.

Ben's Custom Meat Cutting, 6100 Rocky Canyon Rd., Atascadero, CA 93422; 805-466-2103.

Ralph's Custom Meats, 5400 Carrizo Rd., Atascadero, CA 93422; 805-466-2114.

San Joaquin Valley and the Foothills

Lockeford Meats and Sausage, P.O. Box D, Lockeford, CA 95237; 209-727-5584.

Dee's Meat Processing, 10145 Twin Cities Rd., Galt, CA 95632; 209-745-1224.

Los Angeles and Orange Counties

Green Acres Market, 2918 Los Angeles Ave., Simi Valley, CA 93063; 805-526-1312.

Bree's Game Processing, 11877 Valley View Ave., Garden Grove, CA 92845; 714-892-1115.

San Francisco Bay Area

Bobby Lee's Country Smokehouse, 850 Sycamore Ave., Hayward, CA 94544; 510-889-1133.

Madrone Meats, 191 Monterey Rd., Morgan Hill, CA 95037; 408-779-3414.

West Coast Meat Company, 147 Jackson St., Hayward, CA 94544;
510-886-7400

Wild-Pig Cookery

Some people shy away from game meat in general, citing a strong or gamy taste. Others refuse to eat wild game for a number of real or perceived reasons. Generally, wild-game meat, including pork, is low in fat and cholesterol and is considered by doctors and nutritionists to be healthier than beef or domestic pork. Generally, if big-game meat is strong-tasting, it has likely been cared for improperly in the field or is from a male animal taken during the rut (breeding season), when the meat naturally gets strong.

Because feral pigs are not many generations removed from domestic stock, they have maintained some of the milder characteristics that we breed out of wild hogs and into domestic pigs. Compared to deer or elk, wild pork is lighter in color and generally milder in taste. I'm referring here to meat hogs with live weights of 100 to 150 pounds. The meat of a trophy boar that might weigh 300 pounds is going to be tough and likely strong. As previously mentioned, the big boars are best made into sausage, salami, pepperoni, or jerky. The smaller meat hogs are almost always palatable, and a good marinade and recipe will turn even the marginal ones into tasty dishes.

Though the risk is extremely small, wild hogs worldwide can carry trichinosis. For that reason, wild pork should be thoroughly cooked. Here are a number of recipes that I believe do justice to wild pork.

Wild Hog Loin with Mushroom Sauce

2 lb. loin cut into 4 serving-size pieces

1 bottle (12 oz.) Lawry's Red Wine with Cabernet Sauvignon Marinade

1 cup butter or margarine

1 lb. fresh mushrooms, sliced

1 clove garlic, minced

Lawry's Seasoned Salt

Lawry's Garlic Pepper

¼ cup Burgundy wine

In a resealable plastic bag, combine loin and 1¼ cups marinade and refrigerate at least 2 hours or overnight. In large skillet, melt ½ cup butter. Sauté garlic and mushrooms, and set aside. Drain loin and cook in the same skillet until done, adding seasoned salt and garlic pepper to taste. Add Burgundy wine and ¼ cup marinade during the last minute of cooking time. Return mushrooms to the pan to reheat. Remove meat and mushrooms to preheated plates; drizzle with pan juices and roasted pine nuts. Serve with wild rice and your favorite vegetable.

Wild Hog Roast

1 hog roast with bone
4 small to medium onions, chopped
½ pt. sour cream
4 tbsp. beef broth
2 tbsp. margarine
sage, thyme, and marjoram
salt and pepper to taste
flour
1 oz. cognac

Brown roast in margarine in heavy pot. Add onions, salt, and pepper. Season roast with a small amount of sage and other seasonings to taste. Add 4 tbsp. of beef broth. Place covered pot in preheated 300-degree oven. Roast for 1½ to 2 hours, or until roast is done (meat starts to pull away from the bone). Remove meat and strain onions from liquid. Return pan to stove top. Over high heat, add sour cream and a small amount of flour to the remaining liquid to thicken it slightly. Just before serving, add the cognac to the sauce, if desired.

Crockpot Pork

3-4 lb. wild-pig loin roast
2 large onions, sliced
1 clove garlic, minced
salt and pepper to taste
1 tbsp. caraway seeds
1 can beef broth

Place pork into 6-qt. crockpot with all ingredients except caraway seeds. Cook on low for 6 hours. Add caraway seeds and cook for 1 to 2 more hours or until done. Serve over mashed potatoes.

Hunt Club Hog

2 lb. wild-hog meat, cut into 2-in. cubes
¼ cup flour
1 tsp. salt
black pepper to taste
4 tbsp. bacon drippings
1 large onion, cut up
4 small onions, whole
2 cloves garlic, minced
4 potatoes, halved
4 cups water
1 tbsp. parsley flakes

Make a mixture of the flour, salt, and pepper. Coat meat with flour mixture. Brown meat in bacon drippings in a large frying pan, then add cutup onion and garlic. Cook for 5 minutes. Add water and parsley flakes, cover, and cook for 1 to 2 hours until meat is tender. Add potatoes and small whole onions. Cook 30 additional minutes.

Stuffed Pork Tenderloin

2 pork tenderloins of equal size
3 tbsp. chopped onion
¼ cup butter or margarine
4 cups dry bread cut into cubes
¼ tsp. salt
¼ tsp. pepper
½ tsp. poultry seasoning
½ tsp. ground sage
6-oz. can sliced mushrooms
3 tbsp. chicken broth
4 bacon slices

Split tenderloins open lengthwise and flatten. Do not cut through. Cook onion in butter and combine with bread and seasonings. Toss with chicken broth to moisten. Add one 6-oz. can sliced mushrooms, drained. Spread mushroom stuffing over one tenderloin and lay the other on top. Season with salt and pepper and top with bacon slices. Place on rack in open roasting pan. Roast in oven (325 degrees) for 1½ hours.

Smothered Hog Chops

8 chops, ¾ to 1 in. thick
5 bacon slices, cut into ½-in. pieces
½ cup chopped onions
1 clove garlic, minced
2 12-oz. jars mushroom gravy
½ tsp. salt
½ tsp. pepper
1 cup cooked white rice
8 green pepper slices

Fry bacon in a large skillet over medium heat until brown. Remove bacon from skillet and drain on paper towels. Set aside. To the same pan, add chops, onions, and garlic. Brown meat on both sides for 5 to 7 minutes over medium heat. Add mushroom gravy, salt, and pepper. Bring to a boil over medium-high heat. Reduce heat to low, cover, and simmer for 30 minutes. Add cooked rice. Simmer for 35 to 45 minutes or until meat is tender, stirring occasionally. Garnish with bacon and green pepper slices.

Rock-Salt Pork Roast

Small (2- to 4-lb.) pig roast
3 bacon strips, cut into pieces
Black pepper
1 clove garlic
3 to 4 lb. rock salt

Preheat oven to 500 degrees. Make three slits into the roast. Put garlic clove into the middle slit and surround it with pieces of bacon. Pack the rest of the bacon into the two other slits. Sprinkle the roast with pepper. Spread about 1 inch of rock salt in the bottom of a roasting pan and put the roast on top. Pile rock salt around the roast, building it up and using a little hot water as needed to keep the salt in place. Continue piling the salt onto the roast until it is completely covered. Put the roast into the oven, reducing heat to 450 degrees. Bake for 14 minutes per pound.

When you remove the roast from the pan, the rock salt will be very hard and will have to be cracked off with a hammer and chisel. Remove salt pieces and brush off excess salt. Contrary to its name, this roast does not taste salty! The salt brings heat into the meat and yet does not over-salt the roast but rather leaves a crispy coating on the outside.

Wild-Hog Stroganoff

1 lb. hog meat, cubed
¼ cup butter or margarine
1 clove garlic, minced
½ cup onion, chopped
½ tbsp. salt
1¼ cups water
1 cup fresh mushrooms, sliced
1 cup sour cream
flour
pepper

Roll pork cubes in flour and brown in butter with garlic. Add chopped onion, salt, and pepper. Cook 3 to 4 minutes. Stir in water and simmer 30 minutes until tender. Add mushrooms and sour cream and heat but do not boil. Can be served over rice or noodles.

Wild Whiskey Pork Chops

4 to 6 wild-pork chops, ¾ to 1 in. thick
1 medium onion, chopped
1 clove garlic, chopped
1 cup Tarragon vinegar
dash Tabasco and Worcestershire
1 tbsp. hot mustard

⅛ cup chili sauce

½ cup bourbon whiskey

Simmer chops and onion in ¼-in. depth of Tarragon vinegar in a skillet until chops are tender. Add remaining ingredients and stir, cooking over low heat until the mixture is thick. Add a little water or vinegar if needed. When sauce is thick, spread mixture liberally on both sides of the chops, place them in a baking pan, and bake uncovered at 350 for 1½ hours.

Wild-Hog Stew

2 lb. wild pork, cubed

¼ cup flour

4 tbsp. oil

1 medium onion, sliced thin

½ lb. fresh mushrooms

½ cup beef broth

½ cup dry wine

½ tsp. salt

¼ tsp. pepper

1 tbsp. ketchup

1 tsp. Worcestershire sauce

2 tbsp. butter or margarine

3 carrots, cut in 1-in. pieces

6 small red potatoes

1 can stewed tomatoes

Toss meat with flour to coat. Heat oil in large saucepan; brown meat and remove it. Add onion and sauté in butter, then add mushrooms. Add stewed tomatoes, broth, wine, salt, pepper, ketchup, and Worcestershire sauce. Return meat to pan, cover, and simmer 1 hour. Add carrots and small red potatoes, and simmer another hour.

Mesquite Pepper Steak

1 lb. pork round steak ½ in. thick, sliced into 3-inch strips

1½ cups Lawry's Mesquite Marinade with Lime Juice

½ cup flour

½ tsp. Lawry's Seasoned Salt

½ tsp. Lawry's Seasoned Pepper

3 tbsp. vegetable oil

1 large onion, sliced

¾ lb. mushrooms, sliced

1 medium green pepper, cut into thin strips

1 medium red pepper, cut into thin strips

1 tbsp. Worcestershire sauce

1½ cups water

In large resealable plastic bag, combine ¾ cup mesquite marinade and steak; seal bag. Marinate in refrigerator for 2 hours or overnight. Remove steak from bag, discarding used marinade. In another large resealable bag, mix together flour, seasoned salt, and seasoned pepper. Add steak to bag and shake to thoroughly coat with seasoned flour. In a large skillet, heat oil over medium heat. Add steak to hot oil and cook until lightly brown. Stir in onion, mushrooms, peppers, Worcestershire sauce, remaining marinade, and water; mix thoroughly. Reduce heat to low, cover, and cook for 30 to 45 minutes. Stir occasionally. If sauce seems too thick, add a little more water.

Wild Pork Ranchero

4 lb. pork, cubed

½ lb. lean bacon

4 medium onions, chopped

4 medium tomatoes, chopped

2 Anaheim chilies, chopped

2 jalapeno chilies, chopped

2 cloves of garlic, chopped

salt and pepper to taste

¼ cup vegetable oil

½ cup red wine

1 oz. of brandy

Layer bacon slices and meat in large flat frying pan or small roaster. Heat and cook, uncovered, until moisture is all gone (about ½ hour). Do not stir until end of the browning process. Add all other ingredients and stir. Cover and simmer for 1½ to 2 hours. There should be some liquid in bottom. If liquid runs short, add a couple of tablespoons of water or wine after 1 hour. Serve with Spanish rice or noodles.

APPENDIX

There are number of newspapers/newsletters that provide additional information about hog hunting in California.

California Hog Hunter (P.O. Box 9007, San Bernadino, CA 92427; 909-475-1133, e-mail: cahoghunter@earthlink.net) is a monthly newsletter that provides general and where-to-go information about hog hunting in California. The *Hog Hunter* is the only publication devoted entirely to wild-pig hunting in California.

Western Outdoor News (3197-E Airport Loop Dr., Costa Mesa, CA 92626; 714-546-4370, e-mail: wonmail@aol.com) is a weekly sportsman's newspaper available in Northern California and Southern California editions. They provide general and where-to-go information about hunting and fishing in California. They carry wild-hog-hunting information periodically, particularly during the winter and spring.

Fish and Hunting News (P.O. Box 19000, Seattle, WA 98109; 800-488-2827, subscriptions, 206-624-3845, e-mail: staff@fishingandhuntingnews.com) is a bimonthly sportsman newspaper that is available in a California edition. They provide general and where-to-go information about hunting and fishing in California. They carry wild-hog-hunting information periodically, particularly during the winter and spring.

Boar Hunter Magazine (P.O. Box 129, Baxley, GA 31515; 888-297-2627, Web site: www.boarhuntermagazine.com) is a magazine published six times annually that provides how-to and where-to-go information on wild-hog hunting in the United States. *Boar Hunter Magazine* is the nation's only publication committed exclusively to wild-boar hunting.

The Hunting Report (9300 S. Dadeland Blvd., Suite 605, Miami, FL 33156; 305-670-1361, Web site: www.huntingreport.com) is a monthly newsletter that covers where-to-go big-game hunting worldwide. Occasionally, they carry U.S. and California hog-hunting reports.

Guide to Hunting Wild Pigs in California (California Department of Fish and Game, P.O. Box 944209, Sacramento, CA 94299; 916-653-2225) is a booklet revised in 1999 that outlines where to and how to hunt wild pigs in California. It is available free from the Department of Fish and Game.